THE LITTLE BOOK OF

Truffles

Françoise Dubarry
Sabine Bucquet-Grenet

Flammarion

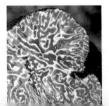

Alphabetical Guide

The alphabetical entries have been classified according to the following categories. Each category is indicated with a small colored square.

■ Environment and Culture

■ Truffle and Truffles

■ Trading and Cuisine

The information given in each entry, together with cross-references indicated by asterisks, enables the reader to explore the world of the truffle.

"To tell the story of the truffle is to tell the history of world civilization," according to the French writer, Alexandre Dumas. We humans have always been fascinated by mushrooms, and especially by the truffle, that strongly fragrant subterranean fungus. Nature deserves its due for having presented us with the black truffle and making it so desirable for its rarity, mystery, and unique qualities. Even to this day, the intricacies of the truffle continue to baffle researchers. This obscurity is part of the truffle's enduring mystique.

The truffle was discovered early in our history, at a time when mankind was seeking out new flavors, culinary refinements, and novel sensations to stimulate the tastebuds. He succumbed to its charms, its succulence, and its heady perfume that is more divine than temporal—and men have been hunting and enjoying truffles ever since.

What Is a Truffle?
Mystery and Magic

The truffle is in fact a fungal growth, but its origins were long the subject of speculation. The Greek philosopher Theophrastus, a disciple of Plato and Aristotle, who specialized in botany, claimed that it was born of a combination of fall rains and dry thunderbolts, and that it was a type of alluvial soil transformed by internal heat. Later theories centered around the cooking of mud aggregates, and everyone believed in the spontaneous generation of these "children of the gods." The medieval Roman Catholic Church long excluded the truffle from celebratory feasts, believing it to be the embodiment of evil. A tubercule that spends its whole life cycle underground, and that is as black as the devil, "as black as the soul of the damned," could not possibly be edible. Poultry, song-birds, furred and feathered game that flew through the sky and lived in the bright light of day, were more noble fare than anything that had a subterranean existence. Then there were the "fairy rings" and the burnt patches around trees created by the truffle, signs that the edible fungus could only be unhealthy.

It was not until the French Revolution that the truffle was restored to its rightful place among the most delicious of foodstuffs: one day of the year was dedicated to a celebration of the truffle's virtues.

Truffle Harvest. Illustration from *Tacuinum sanitatis*, late fourteenth century. Nationalbibliothek, Vienna.

An Obscure Birth

Even though the life cycle of the truffle remained an enigma for centuries, in the early nineteenth century people began to consider how the fungus could be grown under cultivation. Seedlings were infected with mycorrhiza (the "false root" from which the truffle grows). In this way truffle-hunters hoped to observe the fruiting process of this subterranean fungus and elucidate its mysteries. The truffle was found to be the result of a marriage between the mycelium (the network of threads that is the real body of all fungi) and the roots of certain trees; the

Hunting the black truffle. Postcard (1945).

truffle was the fruiting body, created through the exchange of nutrients in this symbiotic association. Despite these advances in knowledge, however, many questions remained unanswered, enabling the truffle to retain its magic and mystique.

The succulent black truffle, usually called the "Périgord truffle" after the region in France where it is found most often, was given the botanical name of *Tuber melanosporum*. Numerous experimental centers were established in the areas of France where the truffle flourished in the wild, in order to see whether it could be produced under cultivation.

THE TRUFFLE THROUGH THE AGES
Early History

Truffles probably featured as a common ingredient of the prehistoric diet. It is more than likely that the cave-dwellers who lived near truffle-bearing oaks were familiar with it. The Romans were wild about truffles, importing them from Libya, Cyrenaica, and Marmarica in sealed jars filled with sand. These were not black truffles, but the white truffle of the genus *Terfez,* which grows in abundance in the desert sands, and was an important component of Babylonian cuisine.

The inhabitants of ancient Gaul lived close to nature, farmed pigs, and hunted wild boar. They considered the black truffle to be a great delicacy. They revered the oak as a holy tree, and the truffle that grew at its feet was considered a gift from heaven. Knowledge of the truffle appears to have disappeared during the Dark Ages and did not reappear until the fourteenth century, when the Burgundy truffle appeared on royal banqueting tables, though this

truffle fell into oblivion in its turn. The white truffle of Alba in Italy was also known at the time and was prepared by Catherine de Medici's Florentine chefs. The white truffle continued to be considered a delicacy until the eighteenth century, though it was not until the nineteenth century that it came into its own.

The Golden Age of Truffles

Wild truffle grounds had always flourished in the huge oak forests that once covered most of Europe, particularly France. Eventually, men learned how to cultivate truffles. In 1808–10, Joseph Talon sowed acorns impregnated with truffle mycelium near the village of Saint-Saturnin d'Apt in south-eastern France, and harvested truffles a few years later. Other growers imitated him, alternating their grape harvests with truffle harvests. When phylloxera devastated vineyards in the late nineteenth century, vines were replaced by truffle-bearing trees in some areas. A huge harvest resulted, and many people still nurture the hope of being able to regain that same level of truffle

Postcard (1945).

273 - En Périgord

Auguste Lançon, *The Truffle Hunter.* Engraving, 1870.

production. From the nineteenth century to the present day, there have been people who have made a living as truffle dealers, selling to restaurants whose menus consists of nothing but truffled dishes. The height of extravagance is a pyramid of whole truffles as a fragrant centerpiece to a dinner table.

Poets and Gourmets

Many nineteenth-century food-writers, gourmets, and poets wrote paeans of praise to this fragrant fungus. The truffle graced the finest tables of the Western world, from elaborate state banquets to

discreet suppers aimed at seduction, and the truffle soon acquired a reputation as an aphrodisiac. The Périgord truffle became the ultimate sign of gastronomic elegance. The French writer Honoré de Balzac slipped it into the menu of the dinners eaten by the characters in his novels. It became the indispensable adjunct to Strasbourg *pâté de foie gras*, which had to be enriched with pieces of raw truffle. In his culinary dictionary, Alexandre Dumas dubbed the truffle *sacro sacrorum* ("holy of holies"). The novelist George Sand served truffles in every type of dish, from the most elegant to the most everyday, from hare *à la royale* to black truffle risotto.

Following double page: The plateau of Valensole.

13

Truffle-hunter on the plateau of Valensole.

THE TRUFFLE INDUSTRY
The Truffle and Truffle-Growers

Until recently, the only truffle cultivated was the Périgord truffle, and then only in France*. Nowadays, attempts are being made to grow this product—pound for pound, probably the most expensive food in the world—outside its native soil. The Périgord truffle still appears to resist cultivation and is capricious to say the least. The truffle needs enormous care if it is to develop a tubercle. It needs just enough warmth, just enough cold spells, just enough rain, a few thunderstorms, a friendly tree, the right kind of soil, the right ecosystem, gentle harvesting, and a skilful cook to bring out the best of the flavor. Once the truffle-growers have

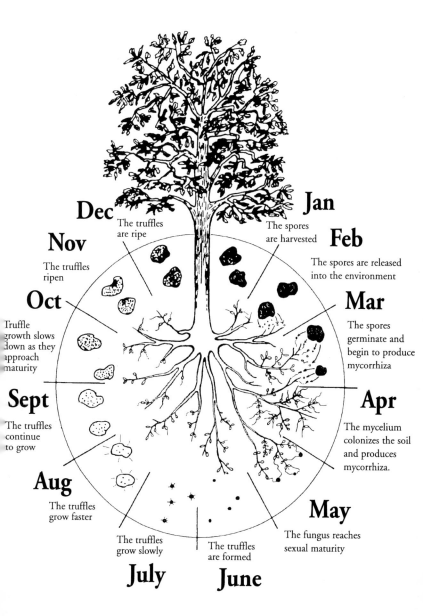

Dec The truffles are ripe

Nov The truffles ripen

Oct Truffle growth slows down as they approach maturity

Sept The truffles continue to grow

Aug The truffles grow faster

July The truffles grow slowly

June The truffles are formed

May The fungus reaches sexual maturity

Apr The mycelium colonizes the soil and produces mycorrhiza.

Mar The spores germinate and begin to produce mycorrhiza

Feb The spores are released into the environment

Jan The spores are harvested

Diagram of the truffle cycle throughout the year

grown their truffles, they then have to deal with a broker* who will take the produce to market. The broker in turn deals with the canner, who preserves truffles and makes them available on the market.

During the golden age of the black truffle, Paris was the main market, and consignments were delivered to the French capital from all over. Thanks to the discovery of heat-treatment for canning* by the Frenchman Nicolas Appert, the black truffle was soon exported all over the world, and the trade flourished.

Truffle-trading is a delicate matter. Those who engage in it are likely to belong to an established family business. The trade is learned on the job, requires a long apprenticeship, and has always worked in the same way. Apart from buying and sorting his wares, the dealer needs to have a good "nose," which means that he needs to be familiar with all the various species of truffle. Most dealers deal only in *Tuber melanosporum* (the black truffle), but there are other truffles that are traded, notably *Tuber aestivum* (the summer truffle) and *Tuber brumale* (the fall truffle), both of which are far less aromatic and thus of much lesser value. Truffle-trading is an exclusive activity. In France, for example, there are only twenty or so truffle-dealers and canners in the whole country.

France is also the main consumer of truffles and produces between twenty and forty tons of the fungus a year (though this figure does not take account of truffles eaten by growers themselves and private sales). It imports a similar amount from Spain* and Italy*, as well as around twenty tons from China*.

Truffles of the World

Tuber melanosporum, the black truffle—also known as the Périgord, Tricastin, or Norcia truffle—grows wild in southwestern and southeastern France. Eastern France produces a truffle that is almost as highly prized, the *Tuber uncinatum*, or Burgundy truffle. Spain and Italy also produce black truffles, though the most famous Italian truffle is the white truffle (*Tuber magnatum*), also known as the Alba or Piedmont truffle. The white truffle is confined almost exclusively to northern Italy, although there are a few acres in neighboring Croatia, which are owned by Italians.

The Bistro de France in Isle-sur-la-Sorgue, Provence.

Attempts are being made to cultivate the black truffle in those parts of the world where other types of truffle already grow wild. These include Slovenia, New Zealand, Tasmania, the northern United States, and even Israel. *Tuber indicum* grows in China and

FRANKREICH (PÉRIGORD).
❖ TRÜFFEL ❖
(Tuber cibarium).

Erklärung siehe Rückseite.

20

the Himalayas and was recently introduced to the Western market. This truffle closely resembles the black truffle but lacks its delicious flavor and, above all, its fragrance, which accounts for the low price. The likelihood that these truffles will be passed off as the genuine article has been alarming truffle-growers and buyers for the past few years.

The Truffle Markets of Europe

Throughout the harvesting* period, which lasts from November through March, the black truffle is sold at local markets*, at which buyers make private deals with sellers. The whole atmosphere is one of utmost secrecy: baskets and small burlap sacks change hands, a few specimens are removed from a pocket. This secrecy befits the mystique of the truffle itself, as hidden in the marketplace as it is in the ground; only the wonderful aroma wafting through the streets betrays its presence in large numbers. Truffle markets are held in several places in southern Europe: most of these events are in France, the largest being at Richerenches*, Valréas, Aups*, and Carpentras, but several towns in Italy also hold their own markets, and particularly truffle festivals, which are becoming ever more popular among tourists. The truffle markets of Spain* are held in the greatest secrecy, sometimes at dead of night*, when truffle-growers come into direct contact with the brokers and dealers.

Flavor and Fragrance

A few top chefs from all over the world, from the United States to New Zealand, have made truffles their specialty trademark, and try to create combinations that enhance the truffle flavor. The black truffle is delicious when eaten raw, but when it is cooked and eaten warm the flavor and fragrance are intensified. The Italian white truffle is usually eaten raw, grated at the last minute for each diner over pasta or risotto. Although the black truffle is also grown in Spain, it is not well-known outside the major cities and there is no culinary tradition of preparation. But whatever the country, the word "truffled" on a menu starts the heart palpitating and sharpens the tastebuds. An entire menu featuring the truffle in all its courses (see Buyer's Guide) might make a hole in your wallet, but you will be guaranteed a once-in-a-lifetime culinary experience: a whole meal based around the "food of the gods."

An advertisement for Liebig Meat Extract, 1897.

ALPHABETICAL GUIDE

■ Alba Truffle Festival

One of the biggest events in the truffling calendar is the annual White Truffle Festival, held at the end of October in the north Italian town of Alba, in the Piedmont region. This long-awaited occasion marks the official start of the truffle-hunting season, and at the auction held on the 31 October (two weeks after the opening) the atmosphere reaches fever pitch as the bidders wait to see whether the prices will beat those of the year before. Prices can reach 400,000 lire per 4 ounces (100 grams) of the finest examples of *Tuber magnatum Pico*, or the Piedmont white truffle.

The festival began in the 1930s, when a tradition began of offering the biggest truffle of the year to a noteworthy figure. Among the lucky recipients were Harry Truman, Marylin Monroe, and Alfred Hitchcock. To this day, the event attracts visitors and top chefs from all over the world. Yet there is always some controversy over whether all the truffles on offer are truly from the region, or whether some are illegal imports from elsewhere. This kind of fraud is inevitable when the demand so outstrips the resources available. The White Truffle Festival remains a highly popular event, and an unparalleled occasion to sample an atmosphere literally saturated with the aroma* of the truffle.

■ American White Truffles

Interest in truffles in the United States began when truffles were first found in 1878 by a certain Dr. H.W. Harkness in California. He gave a paper on

The Truffle Market in Alba, Italy.

Tuber gibbosum Harkn. at the Proceedings of the California Academy of Sciences in 1899, in which he said that American truffles could be compared to European varieties.

Truffles have been cultivated in Oregon since 1986, when the first inoculation took place near Oregon City. Later that year, *Geopora cooperi* was found to be growing exactly where it had been inoculated. The trials continued with Tuber species, and again truffles were found. Sample harvests indicated a production of several hundred pounds per acre. Truffle experts today declare that while nothing quite matches the taste of a genuine wild truffle from Piedmont, cultivated truffles from Oregon are a very acceptable alternative. In particular, it has intense flavor and aroma notes that European truffles are missing. In appearance, it is typically pale and mottled. One of its most attractive features is, of course, its price. It costs less than a tenth of the price of the best Piedmont truffles. American white truffles are especially recommended with pasta, poultry, risotto, gratins, and rabbit.

Béatriz Garrigo,
The Prestigious Aroma of the Truffle.
Ink painting.

AROMA

The fragrance of the truffle has fascinated humans for centuries. It is only recently, however, that research chemists, with the help of mycologists (experts on fungi) and under the auspices of an industrialist, successfully analyzed the aromatic constituents of a fresh black truffle. Scientists have shown that the black truffle* (*Tuber melanosporum*) exudes up to eighty different components, by trapping the atmosphere surrounding freshly unearthed truffles stored in a cold room in order to capture the

smell. Nine constituents were isolated, including dimethyl sulfate. This research made it possible to create an artificial black truffle smell, identical to the natural aroma of the fungus. This product is available on the market in the form of a scented truffle oil. Unfortunately, it is open to misuse, in that it could be used fraudulently to scent "false" truffles that have no culinary value. It is so realistic that the animals used for truffle-hunting—sows, dogs, and even the truffle-fly—are all fooled by the smell. It has even been added to pigswill to make it more palatable. Dogs are also sensitive to this complex aroma, and it is being used to familiarize them with the smell of the truffle as part of the training process. The same research has also made it possible to develop a piece of equipment that will detect the presence of truffles, though the viability of such a truffle gauge has yet to be tested. It was invented in the unlikely setting of Manchester University, England.

French scientists have also developed a quality control standard that makes it possible to differentiate between species of truffle on the basis of the composition of their aroma—a reliable technique for authenticating aromatics. This could contribute to eliminating the practice of palming off "false truffles" on people who know no more about the black truffle than its black, shapeless form.

The village of Aups.

■ Aups

Aups, in southern France, holds one of the best-known truffle markets* in the region, held every Thursday morning from end November to end February. Aups is a typical Mediterranean village, the milky-white bark of the plane trees in the central square mingling with the pastel colors and pale stonework of the painted housefronts. The winter light is sharp and eerie, with the great bare branches of the trees outlined against the cold blue sky. The truffle-growers arrive well before their customers. First they visit the café, or sit under the plane trees, chatting about the previous week's market, about the going rate for truffles, and about the damage done by the Chinese truffle*, whose arrival on the market has appalled producers because the product is so much cheaper, if clearly inferior in quality. There are also worries about the growing Spanish market, whose truffles are being imported and are causing prices to drop. On the

last Sunday in January, to top off the best week for the truffle harvest, the village celebrates "Truffle Day," which attracts visitors from all over the region, and top chefs from even further afield can be spotted, checking the quality of the produce. Many truffle-growers will save their best specimens for the big day. The local restaurateurs replenish their stocks so that they can advertise "all-truffle" menus, using the perfectly ripe, fragrant truffles from Aups and Richerenches*.

■ Benefits of the Truffle

Homage to the truffle, a completely natural food! Truffle cultivation* is truly environmentally friendly. The most recent ecological research shows that the presence of truffles enables the native fauna and flora to flourish. Furthermore, the truffle has taught us that it cannot be intensively cultivated, and the techniques for encouraging its growth are the opposite of those that are used in modern forestry. In fact, the truffle is

Paying homage to the truffle.

at the forefront of attempts to protect the natural environment. It provokes questions and contemplation, and it requires careful nurture of its preferences. It defies the ease of production that is the result of intensive farming and it challenges modern agriculture, which ignored the truffle's needs in order to impose its own. Truffle cultivation encourages tree-planting, helps to prevent soil erosion, and keeps the soil alive. From an agricultural point of view, truffle cultivation contributes to crop diversity and provides a welcome supplementary income in rural areas. It is the only way of preventing the disappearance of the natural truffle-grounds* and it can be reintroduced locally by reviving ancient and traditional cultivation methods. The truffle is also a healthy, slimming food. It contains no fat and has a high water content. It is a vegetable product rich in essential minerals and trace elements, and it was long used in traditional medicine, truffle water being prescribed as an anti-emetic.

■ Black Truffle

The scientific name for the black truffle is *Tuber melanosporum*. This truffle is also known as the Périgord truffle, and less frequently in the English-speaking world as the Tricastin truffle or the Norcia truffle. In Italian it is known as *tartufo nero pregiato*, and in Provence the local name for it is *rabasse*. The black truffle is considered by the French to be the "noble truffle," the most valuable of all the truffles, the one that people seek out in the markets and in gourmet food stores, the one with the most powerful and intense aroma. The ascocarp (the truffle fruiting-body) varies in size from one to four inches, and the peridium (skin) is reddish prior to maturity. The skin is warty and grainy to the touch. The gleba (flesh) is white at first, then marbled and chocolatey-brown upon maturity, with white sterile veining. The aroma is intense but pleasant and distinctive. The fragrance originates from the

30

spores* which release it when the flesh turns dark. When examined under an electron microscope, the spores themselves are seen to be echinulate (covered in short, stiff hairs), and this provides the best means of identifying the species*.

In the same areas as the black truffle is found, other truffles grow that also have a black peridium (skin) and could be mistaken for *Tuber melanosporum.* Chief among these are the musky truffle* (*Tuber brumale*), the summer truffle* (*Tuber aestivum*), the Burgundy truffle* (*Tuber uncinatum*) and *Tuber mesentericum.* All of them have a warty skin and, apart from the summer truffle, all have veined flesh that is dark brown or black in color and is shot through with fine white veins. All have an odor ranging from delicate to strong but that under no circumstances could be said to rival the fragrance of the black truffle. In China, there is a truffle that bears a strong resemblance to the black truffle, especially as it has a warty peridium: the Chinese truffle (*Tuber indicum*). The black truffle grows mainly in Mediterranean Europe: southeastern and southwestern France, the northern half of Italy and the northern half of Spain.

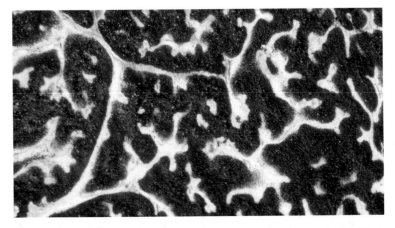

Close-up of marbling on the black truffle.

Bottlers and Canners

Truffle bottling and canning is most often a traditional family business that requires experience, interest, and plenty of practice. It is carried out in a workshop that is equipped with a special machine for brushing the truffles, and industrial canning or bottling equipment. The truffle-canner's skill lies in sorting and grading the truffles and being able to evaluate their quality and provenance. Truffles are supplied to the canner by the broker*, who visits the markets* and needs to buy at the right price. Each bottling and canning businesses uses its regular broker or brokers. Truffles reach the market covered in earth. The first task is to brush them clean, and this is done by hand initially with a special little brush and lots of water, and then with a machine that has a drum fitted with nylon brushes and is fed with pressurized water jets. Once cleaned, the truffles can be identified. This is the sorting process, in which the bottler and canner is an expert. The bottler or the canner slits the skin with a very sharp penknife and checks the marbling of the truffle, enabling him to identify the species. This, together with the appearance of the outer skin and the fragrance, will tell him whether he is dealing with the black truffle* (*Tuber melanosporum*) or a lesser variety. Bottlers and canners need to look out for and reject the musky truffle* (*Tuber brumale*) with its characteristic odor. Merely by determining the thickness of the outer skin, the expert can tell whether a black truffle has come from Italy*, Spain*, or France*. Even if the truffle is a genuine *T. melanosporum*, the canner needs to be extremely selective, on the basis of shape, appearance, size, and maturity, in order to classify the truffle correctly into the categories ("first-choice truffle," "extra," etc.) that are set out in the legislation applying to raw and canned truffles respectively. Raw truffles are sold whole in their outer skins in small baskets made of woven chestnut lathes; they are preserved in bottles or cans. Truffles are sterilized by placing them in cans with a little water and salt. They lose twenty-five per cent of their weight during the sterilization process.

Brokers

As the principal customer for the truffle-grower's wares, the truffle-broker is the key figure in the truffle trade. Brokers act as the agent in all the commercial transactions; they visit the markets and make purchases on behalf of dealers, bottlers and canners*, and wholesalers, but they do not sell to individuals. Each "truffle house" has its own favorite broker or brokers. They heavily influence the going rate, which is based on availability and demand, and they buy at the best possible price in order to assure their mark-up. Depending on the region, the brokers come by their supplies in various ways, according the requirements of their customers. They call on the growers, or the growers may come to visit them. They also buy at the best-known wholesale markets. Even so, part of the truffle production escapes both the broker and the market. It is extremely difficult to evaluate the amount of home consumption by growers and the number of direct sales to individuals who have established relationships with growers, but is believed at least to be equivalent to the official production figures.

Reliable statistics for production and consumption are difficult to come by. Only twenty-five percent of growers account for some three-quarters of truffles purchased "over the counter." The custom is to pay for truffles in cash, which is why so many deals are observed in which the participants gather around the trunk of an automobile and bundles of notes change hands in the open air.

Brokers have to be able to judge quality in an instant: if the broker is in doubt about, say, whether a truffle is a *Tuber brumale* or a *melanosporum*, he will surreptitiously insert his thumbnail into the truffle's outer skin in order to reveal the flesh, whose color and veins indicate the species* and the degree of maturity.

Brokerage is a seasonal activity, which lasts throughout the winter. At other times of year, some brokers deal in the summer truffle*, *Tuber aestivum* and in antoher regional delicacy—dried mushrooms, such as morels and cepes. They may engage in other occupations that are related to farming, and some brokers are even truffle-growers.

A broker weighing truffles.

■ BURNT PATCH

The term "burnt patch" refers to the circular bare patch that surrounds certain truffle-bearing trees. It is bare of vegetation and is the same phenomenon that is observable in the spring in grassland where the Fairy Ring Champignon (*Marasmius oreades*) grows. Fairy rings or burnt patches indicate that a fungus mycelium is flourishing underground. At first, the vegetation around the tree gradually disappears, but a few plants nevertheless stubbornly linger on. Pierre Sourzat, a truffle expert, calls these "indicators" that "favor" truffle growth. The fungus Sheep's fescue (*Festuca ovina L.*) is an excellent companion for the truffle, since it attracts sheep whose little pellets of dung are particularly nourishing for the truffle fruiting body. The truffle mycelium* alone is not capable of creating a burnt patch. Green plants that are attracted to the area, such as the mouse-ear hawkweed, have herbicidal properties. The burnt patch that betrays the presence of the black truffle* (*Tuber melanosporum*) may not lie right under an

oak-tree; the mycorrhized root may grow away from the tree with time. In some places, the burnt patch is less obvious as it is often invaded by couch-grass. The burnt patch produced by the dog-nose truffle (*Tuber rufum*) is more clearly defined than that produced by the black truffle (*T. melanosporum*); the Burgundy truffle* (*Tuber uncinatum*), on the other hand, produces a burnt patch that is barely visible, as it

grows in the undergrowth; the summer truffle* (*Tuber aestivum*), a species that grows further north, produces a crescent-shaped burnt patch, and the musky truffle* (or fall truffle, *Tuber brumale*) produces an almost invisible patch.

The burnt patch does not mean that the fungus has the better part of the bargain in the relationship between the truffle and the host tree. It is a matter of an exchange, although much mystery still surrounds the symbiosis between the two plants and the way in which nutrients pass from tree to fungus and back. The tree supplies vitamins and carbon, the truffle procures nitrogen, phosphorus, water, and mineral salts.

Above: a "fairy ring."
Left: the largest burnt patch ever found, some 73 feet or 24 meters in diameter.

Burgundy Truffle

Tuber uncinatum.

The Burgundy truffle (*Tuber uncinatum*) grows exclusively in the wild, mainly in central-eastern France, though it is also found in Switzerland, Belgium, the Netherlands, Luxemburg, Germany, and even Russia. Unlike the sun- and heat-loving Périgord truffle (black truffle*), it prefers a cool soil* and shady conditions. This truffle is rounded or irregular in shape, ranging in size from a walnut to an apple. The peridium is warty, and turns blackish-brown on maturity. The gleba is firm, dark brown veined with white. The flesh is gray prior to maturity, which has caused the Burgundy truffle to be called the "gray truffle," though this name is considered unattractive and has been rejected by truffle producers. The truffle has the delicate fragrance of hazelnut and a very pleasant flavor. When eaten raw it retains all of its perfume. The Burgundy truffle is harvested in France from September 15 through January 31, and production varies between seven and fifteen metric tons a year, though just over a century ago, it yielded as much as 178 metric tons. Until the Renaissance, it was the only truffle to be served at royal banquets. The Burgundy truffle is beginning to regain market share, thanks to the efforts currently being made, in particular by organisations representing truffle farmers. Restaurateurs have also lent their support to the campaign: the Burgundy truffle is coming into its own again thanks to talented chefs who use the raw truffle as an aromatic in the same way as the Italian white truffle is used, grated over hot pasta dishes.

■ CELEBRATING THE TRUFFLE

Several events are organized annually in Europe and North America in honor of the truffle. Most of them are run by special organizations formed to promote and defend the mysterious *Tuber melanosporum* in the eyes of the public and the media; often the local tourist authority lends a hand, recognizing the growing popularity of such events. Especially dedicated are the Truffle Brotherhoods, Confréries, or Confraternità, who promote the truffle with ceremonial costumes and obscure rites, mostly for the publicity value, though there is no doubt that members are also fervent truffle-worshippers. The rituals are conducted with great solemnity, and the participants wear the regalia of their order. The Confrérie du Diamant Noir (Black Diamond Brotherhood) maintains a choir that takes part in the famous Richerenches* Mass (see Religion), held in honor of Saint Anthony*, the patron saint of the truffle-growers.

Initiation rite into the Confrérie de la Truffe Noire.

Each order has its own induction ceremony, but all are accompanied by truffle-hunts and sumptuous feasts, during the course of which the candidate is introduced to the company and swears an oath of loyalty and devotion to the divine tubercule. New orders are created almost every year, and even the oldest has only existed since the 1980s.

In the United States, a White Truffle Festival is held annually in different cities, bringing the good news about truffles to the whole country.

Chinese Truffles

The first recorded farming of fungus in China dates back to the seventh century. Chinese truffles are gathered from November through March, and have always been a valuable food for country dwellers during the winter months when other sources of nourishment are rarer. It is sold in stores in various forms: dried in strips, preserved whole in salt, or fresh. In some producing areas, such as Yongsheng in northern Yunnan, the truffle is so abundant that the locals eat it as an ordinary vegetable. Yunnan truffles have deep black meat, and can weigh as much as seven ounces (180 grams). Pigs were traditionally used to detect truffles, but nowadays truffles are usually dug up by hand.

The Chinese truffle is almost identical in appearance to the black truffle* (*Tuber melanosporum*), with a very similar blackish-brown, warty peridium, though the warts are slightly smaller than in *T. melanosporum*. The gleba is purplish black when mature and is shot through with white veins. These are more numerous than in the black truffle and do not turn red on exposure to the air as do the veins in the black truffle. The truffle is found on the slopes of the Himalayas west of Tibet, in the provinces of Sechuan and Yunnan, in pine woods or growing among morels, pine boletes, and matsutake, a mushroom of which the Japanese are particularly fond.

Although Chinese produce is generally considered inferior in Europe and North America, companies are beginning to export local produce to the West, where they are able to undercut the high prices charged for the best produce and thus obtain an increasingly noticeable share in the market. The Chinese truffle is mild in flavor, which makes it much less valuable in culinary terms. The best way to tell Chinese truffles from *T. melanosporum* (and thus to avoid paying over the odds) is to look at the truffle under a magnifying glass. The bumps on the truffle's surface should be gently rounded. Pointed, triangular bumps are the sign of the Chinese truffle.

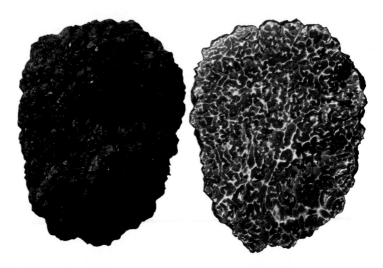

■ Choosing a Truffle

It is very hard to be certain of buying a good black truffle* (*Tuber melanosporum*) in the market, when it is sold caked with earth, unbrushed, and unwashed. It can come in a variety of shapes and sizes, though this has no effect on the quality. However, a medium-sized or large truffle makes better eating than a small one, because of the quantity of flesh. Average or larger truffles are also easier to cut into paper-thin slices, whereas small ones can be broken or chopped for combining with scrambled eggs, in the time-honored tradition. A truffle that has been gnawed by a field-mouse or damaged by an earthworm or small red beetle is still perfectly edible but sells at a much lower price.

The quality of truffles varies from year to year and can be measured by the intensity of the aroma, which is itself an indication of the maturity. It is preferable to do the buying soon after Christmas, when the season is at its peak. The only deciding factor for a truffle, whether the black or the white variety, is the aroma*. To judge this, it is advisable to close the eyes and hold the truffle close to the nose. The black truffle has an unmistakable odor, delicate but overwhelming, and the odor of the white truffle* is overpowering. If the truffle is odorless or if it has a grassy smell, it may be the musky truffle* (*Tuber brumale*). This species can be smuggled into batches of black truffles thanks to its very dark, warty outer skin, which closely resembles that of its superior cousin, the *T. melanosporum*. The next step is to examine the outer skin (the peridium). Touch it and ensure that it is firm; never buy a soft truffle. If you get the chance, scratch the skin discreetly with a fingernail to ensure that it is not frozen. Truffle-growers, canners*, and brokers* alike usually make a tiny slit with a penknife into the flesh of the truffle that helps to identify the quality and species*. The worst that can happen is that a "false truffle" has been smuggled into the batch, namely the Chinese truffle* (*Tuber*

Applying forestry principles to truffle cultivation.

indicum) that so closely resembles the black truffle, outside and in. The Chinese truffle is very mild in flavor, and thus much less appreciated. It takes a lifetime to be able to recognize the geographical origin of the true black truffle, and only experts can do it. One piece of good news is that there is no difference in flavor between truffles that occur naturally in the wild and those that grow as the result of inoculation with mycelium.

Cultivation (Trufficulture)

Truffle cultivation originated in southeastern France in the nineteenth century. A certain Joseph Talon got the idea of sowing acorns in calcareous soil. The young oaks that grew in this soil, which was already saturated with truffle spores, proved to be excellent truffle producers. Once proved to be successful, the pratice was repeated on a larger scale around 1880, when French

vineyards were ravaged by the phylloxera plague. Cultivation reached a peak at the turn of the century, but was cut short by the First World War. The exodus from the countryside, coupled with the huge loss of life, and the subsequent mechanization of agriculture ruined the truffle industry. It was not until the 1980s that truffle culture was revived. It has made considerable progress, thanks to the widespread availability of seedlings mycorrhized by *Tuber melanosporum* as well as through the excellent work of agricultural research centers. Several methods of artificial cultivation have been tried, some of which are used in the field. The traditional method is still used in some regions. This consists in planting in limestone soil truffle-bearing trees that are not inoculated with mycorrhiza*. They are carefully nurtured, the soil is cleared of vegetation, and the trees are regularly trimmed and pruned.

The Pallier method makes use of mycorrhized trees that are planted in a grove, and the soil is tended as for forestry. The first truffles appear between five and ten years later. The Tanguy method also involves planting mycorrhized trees, but in this case other plant-life is allowed to flourish alongside. The first truffles are harvested between ten and twelve years later. Despite the development of all these techniques, the black truffle is becoming rarer, and this trend has been noticed over the last few decades. Some people claim that applying forestry methods to truffle-growing is wrong, and that human intervention using modern agricultural methods has created conditions whereby the natural fauna and flora are eradicated, to the detriment of the fungus` development. The truffle is the result of the interaction of three interdependent factors—the soil, the climate, and the biosphere. Today, truffle-growers are trying to reconcile the innovations suggested by scientists with traditional know-how. Even though great strides have been made in research, truffle cultivation remains a subsidiary occupation for most farmers, who are all too aware of its seasonal nature and its labor-intensiveness.

Truffle-hunting with man's best friend.

■ Dog

Truffle-hunting* with a dog is an ancient tradition. There are many advantages to hunting with these animals. They are docile, very mobile, have an infallible sense of smell and can be bought for a fair price despite their valuable skills. Furthermore, they are often deeply attached to their owners and will hunt for truffles

purely to please them, even though the dogs reap no direct benefit from the activity. Dogs do, however, need to be trained to seek out truffles, since in normal circumstances the smell does not hold any particular appeal for them. It is therefore essential to train a dog to identify the aroma. Then the animal needs to be given an incentive to find the fungus, and finally, it must learn how to work consistently and reliably. There is no question that the truffle-hound can perform miracles when it comes to seeking out the divine fungus. It can unearth ripe truffles without damaging those that are not yet ripe, but it will come back and find them as they ripen. Of course, such a result cannot be achieved without a long period of training and a little patience and psychology. It is all a question of the bond between the owner and the animal. The hound, nose to the ground to sniff out the odors percolating from underground, methodically explores the truffleground. It goes back and forth until it marks with his paw the place where it scents a truffle. The hunter can then gently remove the fungus and provide a suitable "reward" for the companion that has worked so hard. Any breed of dog can be used as a truffle-hound, but certain breeds have gained a particularly good reputation in this area. They include dachshunds, alsatians, spaniels, and labradors. Gun-dogs should be avoided, however, as they may be distracted by the scent of game. Truffle-hound trials have come into fashion, and these truffle-hunting competitions attract dog-lovers and truffle-hunters alike.

■ Experimentation

For the past decade and a half, groups of scientists from all over the developed world have

An experimental plantation.

The fall truffle.

promoting truffle growth on a truffle-producing tree. They conduct experiments on various species of Tuber and have embarked on a special study of *Tuber uncinatum*, the Burgundy truffle*, which does not respond to the same cultivation methods as the black truffle* (*Tuber melanosporum*).

Much of this research takes place in southwestern France, which is real truffle country. Perhaps more surprisingly, Manchester University in northern England has also been involved in developing an electronic "nose," a truffle-detector that senses the presence of tubers underground.

■ Fall Truffle

Two truffles mature in the fall: the white truffle* of Alba and Piedmont and the Burgundy truffle*. The first (*Tuber magnatum*) is highly prized in Italy, almost the only country in which it grows, and fetches an extraordinarily high price*. Production amounts to between five and thirty metric tons. The peridium is smooth, dirty yellow in color and slightly slimy to the touch. The gleba is white to reddish-brown, veined with white. This truffle is harvested from October through December, mainly in northern and central Italy. It has a strong odor of garlic, shallot, and sharp cheese, these being echoed in the mouth. It is eaten raw, grated over pasta or risotto. The Burgundy truffle (*Tuber uncinatum*) is closely related to the summer truffle*. Its peridium consists of a series of little scales, and the gleba is chestnut brown at maturity, with thin, ramified white veining. The odor recalls that of undergrowth, and in the mouth the flavor

worked hard to develop truffle cultivation*. The results are promising, so Italy* is now trying to improve production of its white truffle* and its black truffle*. Some research is also being performed in Spain*, though the results have yet to be made public. A European Tuber Group has been formed to promote the exchange of knowledge between countries and to evaluate the current experiments. Agricultural chambers of commerce and local authorities are also involved in the regions where the work is being done. About fifty scientists are working full-time on experimentation and training. They have a very wide remit, involving the definition of a suitable truffle-producing sapling and its reaction to mycorrhyzation, a study of the relationship between the truffle and the soil and the truffle and the climate, and the best techniques for

resembles that of a hazelnut. It is harvested from October through January, yielding between seven and eight metric tons a year. The production area is located in eastern France, in the regions of Burgundy, Lorraine, Franche-Comté, and Champagne. Italy also produces *T. uncinatum* in the province of Emilia-Romagna. It is usually eaten raw, as it loses its flavor when cooked.

Tuber mesentericum, the mesenteric truffle, has a very dark peridium that is covered in tiny warts, and the fungus is deeply grooved. It smells strongly of phenol and has a bitter taste. It is found in Normandy, England, the Czech Republic, and central Germany.

Tuber borchii, the bianchetta truffle, looks and smells like the white "Alba" truffle. It is harvested mainly in Italy and in Provence. It is strongly scented, and the Italians call it the poor man's white truffle.

Tuber macrosporum is another Italian white truffle and, like the Alba truffle, it smells of garlic, but it is of no culinary interest.

■ Finding Truffles

The operation of unearthing a truffle is as delicate as it is unpredictable. The truffle is better detected by creatures

Truffle-hunting dog trials at Forcalquier in France.

such as dogs and pigs, whose sense of smell is more refined than that of humans. Truffle-hounds (see Dog), pigs* (especially sows) and truffle-flies* are used for this purpose. Each of these animals has its disadvantages, and so scientists have invented an electronic truffle detector. Although this is still at an experimental stage (at Manchester University, England), it has proved extremely reliable, although its use would be restricted to small areas. Truffle-hunting methods vary depending on local tradition in different regions. It is decades since truffle-hunters* had to rely solely on their eyesight to spot a truffle patch and then unearth the fungus from beneath a few inches of soil. It is all a question of odor, and because the sense of smell is relatively poorly developed in humans, the hunter needs a more gifted companion. The truffle-hunter thus covers the truffle-grounds* accompanied by a dog or a pig, depending on the region. The French, Italians, and Spaniards often prefer dogs, who do not particularly like truffles but enjoy seeking them out since they know they will be rewarded with food that they like better. In some regions, such as Périgord, the pig is used. Its sense of smell is as keen as that of a dog but, unlike the hound, it adores truffles. The problem lies therefore not so much in training the pig to sniff out the truffles as in getting it to relinquish the prize to its master, conquering its instinct for gluttony—rather a challenge given the size and determination of a fully-grown sow! Some experts try to locate the truffle-fly which locates the truffle by smell and hovers above it to inhale the perfume, since it lays its eggs inside the truffle. Whichever animal is chosen for the task, once the truffle has been located, man must intervene by helping the animal to dig out the fungus by means of a special truffle-unearthing tool.

■ France

Joseph Talon invented truffle cultivation at the beginning of the nineteenth century, but it was not until the end of that century that the truffle experienced its golden age in France. This was when the phylloxera plague destroyed most of the French vineyards, so grape-growers replaced their damaged vines with pubescent oaks, having noted that this tree did particularly well on the dry limestone plateaux typical of the Mediterranean basin, producing an abundance of truffles where once grapes had grown. The truffle harvest brought great wealth to the planters in the regions of Périgord, Quercy, and southeastern France. However, during the First World War the general exodus from the countryside and the huge loss of life caused the truffle-grounds to become neglected and production to fall steeply. Later, the intensive agriculture practiced after the Second World War exacerbated this decline. Truffle-bearing trees were no longer cultivated and the truffle-grounds were tilled with the same agricultural machinery that was used on cereals, causing serious harm to the mycorrhizal root system. For the past fifty years, France has been trying to repair the appalling damage suffered by the truffle-growing industry, and much is now being done to secure the future* of production. Teams of scientists are constantly striving to improve the productivity of mycorrhized seedlings, and agricultural research stations dedicated to the truffle have been set up in the truffle-growing regions.

The principal regions of France that produce truffles are in the southern half of the country. The southeast (the three regions of Rhône-Alpes, Languedoc-Roussillon, and Provence-Côte-d'Azur) is responsible for between eighty-five and ninety-five percent of national production of *Tuber melanosporum* and *Tuber brumale*, while the southwest (the regions of Aquitaine, Midi-Pyrénées, Poitou-Charente, and Limousin) produces the rest. There is also some production of the Burgundy truffle in the central eastern region. Production in the 2000-2001 season was approximately forty metric tons, about the same as for 1997–1998. French truffle production continues to lag way behind demand, so France needs to import black truffles from abroad, mainly from Spain and Italy.

Example of a truffle reconstituted with matchsticks.

■ FRAUD

There is plenty of incentive for fraud in the truffle industry. The incredibly high prices fetched by truffles, the lean years in which the yield is poor, and the ignorance of consumers who cannot distinguish between the species or recognize the fragrance all conspire to create a tempting environment for the fraudster. There are the old tricks of putting truffles of an inferior type at the bottom of a basket filled supposedly with *Tuber melanosporum*, or of sprinkling artificial truffle flavoring over other dark-colored fungi such as the horn of plenty, or even over black seaweed. Then there are those who use walnut juice to blacken the interi-

or of the summer truffle* (*Tuber aestivum*) or the *terfez**, both of which are white. Another ruse consists of selling unripe truffles, such as those "marked" and stolen by poachers from truffle-grounds as early as September, before they have had a chance to mature. Such truffles are later blackened artificially and even injected with truffle-juice. Deep-frozen truffles are also defrosted and sold as fresh. Other tricks include selling earth-encrusted lumps of coal and earth-encrusted cypress cones (highly poisonous!), as well as pieces of truffle held together with matchsticks or toothpicks. Theft is not fraud, strictly speaking, and mostly involves gathering truffles from a cultivated truffle-ground without the owner's permission. Theft from cultivated grounds is a punishable offense, but in southeastern France and in Italy, there is a certain amount of tolerance in regard to gathering truffles from wild truffle-grounds. In Périgord, however, the truffle is sacrosanct wherever it is found. To combat fraud, the French National Truffle Federation has suggested regulating the season, which would vary depending on the region, while in Toulouse, scientists have identified the components of the aroma* of the black truffle* and the truffle spores* specific in appearance to each species, so any "intruders" can be verified under the microscope.

■ Fresh, Bottled or Canned?

Should truffles be eaten fresh or canned? Due credit should be given to the virtues of the fresh truffle. The quality of the fresh truffles that are on sale from November through March is vastly superior to that of canned or perserved truffles. What makes the fresh *Tuber melanosporum* or black truffle* so special is its extraordinary fragrance, which will send anyone who encounters it for the first time into raptures. The aroma* is powerful, intense, and pervasive. It floats over the truffle markets* and is all-powerful from the moment the truffle is unearthed, lingering for several days wherever it is left, and perfuming every food with which it is cooked. Ideally, a raw truffle should be eaten within three or four days of purchase. Canned and bottled truffles have been cooked and though they last longer, their fragrance is diminished. Those truffles that have been heat-treated only once retain some fragrance, but those that are heat-treated twice (as the legislation requires if they are to be sold to food manufacturers who use them in their preparations) lose their flavor and are barely recognizable as the black truffle, *T. melanosporum.*

■ Future of the Truffle

The black truffle* (*Tuber melanosporum*), continues to worry the truffle-growing world, which has still not been able to halt the invasion of the black truffle grounds by the more successful but less fragrant musky truffle* (*Tuber brumale*).

In recent years, there has been a major drive to increase truffle production and introduce truffle cultivation* in places where it was hitherto unknown, such as North America (see American White Truffles), New Zealand, Tasmania, and even Israel. Many research and experimentation* centers have been set up to promote the cultivation of the black truffle. Events, festivals, and markets are organized. The European Commission supports

programs to promote trufficulture* and encourage trade between France, Spain and Italy. France, for instance, plants an average of 400,000 mycorrhized seedlings a year, and more and more young people all over Europe and even in North America are taking an interest in truffle-growing as a career. Scientific and agricultural institutions have pioneered the innoculation of seedlings with fungal mycorrhiza, and techniques have improved considerably over the past thirty years. According to research, certain truffle plantations of artificially-inoculated seedlings are producing yields that equal those traditional areas. What will happen to the prestige of *T. melanosporum* if the Chinese truffle* (*Tuber indicum*), a species which resembles it closely in everything but taste and aroma, ignores the legislation that governs the trade and invades the market at low prices?

The future of truffle-growing depends largely on regular,

attained in the early twentieth century. Spain and Italy, which have traditionally had truffle-growing regions, are also expanding production. Truffle-growers from countries with a tradition of trufficulture are beginning to be worried about imports and competition from outside the dependable yields, and these are still uncertain. If the problems are overcome and growers are able to produce enough truffles to support a healthy international trade, then the truffle's fate is assured—whether supplies come from traditional European sources or further afield.

Truffle and sweet potato with baby spring vegetables.

"When I eat truffles, I become livelier, gayer, more amenable; inside me, especially in my veins, I feel a voluptuous, gentle warmth that soon communicates itself to my head."

Alexandre Dumas, *Grand Dictionnaire de cuisine*

Certain chefs have produced signature truffle dishes—and not just in France: special truffle menus are offered in restaurants from Texas to New Zealand. Not all chefs prefer the black truffle*. *Tuber melanosporum* is the first choice with scrambled eggs, but the white truffle*, *Tuber magnatum*, is the favorite with pasta and risotto, while the summer truffle*, *Tuber aestivum*, is sprinkled generously over potato salad and green salads. *Tuber uncinatum*, the Burgundy truffle*, whose reputation is as high as that of the black truffle, is delicious grated into a dish of green salad with chicken gizzards.

Should truffles be eaten cooked or raw? All the experts agree, the truffle does not benefit from cooking. Whether white or black, the intensity of the perfume and flavor is only retained in the raw truffle. Italians would never, under any circumstances, cook their truffles. Crunching morsels of truffle in the mouth remains a sublime moment. Truffle recipes should be as simple as possible. A raw truffle should be sprinkled with olive oil and salt and eaten with steamed or boiled potatoes, fettuccini, or scrambled eggs. The skin should not be peeled, nor should the truffle be washed, but if carefully brushed it will have the faint, piquant aftertaste of the earth from which it came, attesting to its origin. Dedicated truffle-lovers will only contemplate consuming dishes incorporating the black truffle, *T. melanosporum,* and the white truffle, *T. magnatum*, both of which are the peak of excellence, with the local wines of the region in which they grow.

Truffles have always been a luxury food and have aroused passions before and after cooking. The Roman gourmet Apicius, King Louis XIV of France, the Italian composer Rossini, King Edward VII of England, and many others have enjoyed consuming them in sophisticated dishes.

In the cultivated truffle-grounds, the first harvest does not occur until the eighth or ninth year, three or four years after the burnt patch* first appears. When harvesting is in full swing, the truffles need to be unearthed in dry weather, and sometimes harvesting has to be delayed for ten or twenty days if the weather is poor. The truffle-grower must inspect the truffle-beds methodically several times a week—partly to deter poachers—but the truffles do not need to be harvested more frequently than once a week. Freshly gathered, raw truffles will keep for no longer than five to eight days, and if they are destined for the market, they are dug up on the preceding day. Overripe truffles are immediately reburied under truffle-bearing trees to serve as "seed-truffles."

■ Harvesting

In the early twentieth century, about one thousand metric tons of truffles were gathered in France, but today the harvest amounts to only twenty to forty metric tons, and even then, only in a "good" year. It is hard to evaluate the yield of a truffle-ground*, since it varies from region to region and season to season, and depends as much on the health of the truffle-ground as on its environment and the prevailing weather conditions. Harvesting begins in late November and ends around the end of February or early March. Although mid-December is considered to be the "high season," the best truffles are unearthed from mid-January through mid-February.

■ Hunters

Of all the trades associated with the truffle, the truffle-hunter gains most from the fungus. Hunters dig out the truffle with the help of a truffle-hound* or other companion. The highlight of a truffle-hunting excursion is when the hound gets the scent, meaning that he has sniffed the aroma of a ripe truffle. Other aids to harvesting are the pig*, or rather the sow, especially in southwestern France*, and the truffle-fly*, the latter being an indicator that truffles are present. The use of pick-axes for unearthing truffles has been forbidden for centuries in many regions because of the damage they do, but they are used on the slopes of the Himalayas for harvesting the Chinese truffle* (*Tuber indicum*). French, Italian, and Spanish truffle-hunters have an detailed knowledge of the local countryside that enables them to spot the signs that indicate where truffles may be growing. They watch the heavens and the earth, look out for burnt patches* on the soil around a host tree, study the local rainfall, the sun, the moon*, and even the air; they grab a handful of soil and sniff it, and know a thousand tricks for seeking out the presence of the divine truffle and exposing the rare fungus. It is so hard to detect that it leaves the hunter in suspense until the last possible moment: Is it the genuine article? Is it large or small? Is it fully ripe? Even if the find is not up to expectations, the hunter can always come back tomorrow— in secret, of course. No truffle-hunter will reveal the mysteries of the hunt: they each have their own way of finding "the black diamond" beneath their feet. The unearthing implement used by truffle-hunters varies depending on the region, but it is always small, in order to do as as little damage as possible to the surrounding earth and underground mycelium. It may be a stick, an iron bar, a little pick, or an asparagus gouge, or a even small metal implement specially designed for the task.

■ Italy

Italy has always had a great tradition of hunting and eating truffles. As early as the ninth century, the white Piedmont truffle was served at the Pope's table, and the Italians greatly revere and honor their native truffle. The main production region extends from northern to central Italy. The truffle-grounds* are mainly natural (Italy never suffered from the phylloxera plague of the vines which led to truffle cultivation in France), although since the 1980s, Italy has been involved in a major program of planting truffle-bearing trees, arranging meetings with the other major truffle-producing countries of Europe, conducting research, and setting up experimenta-tion* centers. The nine truffles that Italy recognizes as suitable for sale are the same as those recognized in France. Fifteen regions produce not only *Tuber magnatum*, the white truffle*, but the black truffle*, *Tuber melanosporum* (Norcia) and the summer truffle*, *Tuber aestivum*. An association of eighteen towns and cities, the

Village near Rieti, Italy, a truffle-producing area.

Città del tartuffo, organizes truffle festivals and wonderful markets*, the best known of which, the *Fiera Nationale del Tartuffo di Alba*, centers around the white truffle. It is held in Alba*, which also has a national truffle museum. There is legislation governing the trade in truffles and the dates on which they can be harvested. Truffle-gathering is permitted on wild truffle-grounds but not on cultivated ones, which are clearly indicated and signposted. Each *trifolau* (truffle-hunter*) must have a licence, has to hunt with a dog* or a pig*, and is required to close up the hole left by their dig and smooth down the surrounding earth.

Despite the fact that Italy produces almost as many truffles as France, it imports truffles from France and Spain to satisfy its internal market, supplemented by truffles from Slovenia and Croatia (which were once part of Italy) and from as far afield as China. It exports its own truffles—and in particular the much-prized white truffle—all over the world, but mainly to Europe.

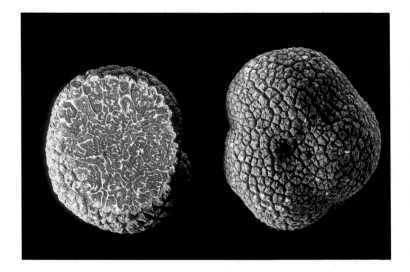

"Truffle" is the common name given to all hypogeous (or underground) fungi as opposed to epigeous fungi, whose fruiting bodies emerge above ground. Most of the hypogeous fungi belong to the family of Ascomycetes, so-called because the spores are contained in an *ascus* (or sac), though there is a variety of white truffle called Elaphomyces that belongs to the family of Basidomycetes, whose spores grow on club-shaped excrescences. All truffles grow from a mycelium* that lives in symbiosis with the roots of certain trees; they cannot survive without this host tree. The exact life cycle of the truffle remains a matter for conjecture, and the first stages of its formation are little known. Does it form in contact with the mycorrhiza*, from strands of mycelium that escape from the root? No one knows exactly what happens from March through May. As soon as the truffle forms, it becomes autonomous, but what does it live on? It puts on a spurt of growth from August through September. Its peridium (skin), which consists of a series of warts, is reddish at this time of year. It ripens in the soil from December through March. The gleba (flesh) is black-to-violet when mature and is marbled with white veins representing a network of filaments of sterile mycelium. It is in the dark flesh that the *asci* (sacs) form that hold the fertile spores*. Three conditions are needed for its cultivation: the right type of soil*, a host, and the right climate. There is a potential for production in spring, but this dwindles later in the season*, especially if it does not rain at exactly the right time. Truffles are classified by genus (mostly *Tuber*) and by species (such as *melanosporum*), but not by variety.

Tuber indicum, the Chinese truffle.

Markets

For anyone interested in truffles, at least one visit to a truffle market is a must. The atmosphere is most unusual and very special. It is best to arrive well in advance and head for the local café. There you can listen to the gossip, enter into conversation, discover what people have to say (in the hope that they reveal something interesting), watch for any transactions taking place, and absorb the fascinating truffle fragrance in the air, which arrives with the first baskets carried in by the truffle-hunters. Their wrinkled and sun-burned faces indicate that they have lived most of their lives outdoors, and their callused hands pay testimony to their daily contact with the soil. Murmuring secretively among themselves, they have a conspiratorial air as they discuss the prices their wares are likely to fetch that day. Truffle-markets are enjoying ever greater success, as they attract truffle-lovers in search of authenticity and fresh produce.

Each market has its own rites, opening ceremony, and hours and days of operation. The markets are all picturesque, but some are larger than others,

The Lalbenque truffle market.

The Cahors truffle market.

depending on the surrounding production area and the help they get from the local authorities. Most are wholesale markets, though a few specialize in selling to individuals.

The most important and best-known French truffle markets are held at Aups*, Valréas, Richerenches*, Carpentras, and Lalbenque. Markets are also held in Burgundy to promote the sale of the Burgundy truffle*, but they do not have regular opening days. Burgundy truffles tend to be sold directly to restaurateurs and caterers (seventy-five percent) with only a minority going to individuals (twenty-five percent).

Italy also has truffle markets, very similar in ambience to the French ones, in small towns in the north of the country, from November to March. The best advice is to contact the town's tourist office to see when the market takes place. The most important truffle-related event in Italy is, of course, the White Truffle Festival, held annually in the town of Alba.

59

La Lune.

Moon

If the experience of several generations of truffle-growers is to be believed, the moon has an influence on the production of truffles. Some growers and hunters are certain that between the full moon and the last quarter, more truffles are ripe for picking. Some believe, on the basis of their experiences in August, that there is also a relationship between the amount of rainfall and the full moon during that month. Geologists claim that there is no statistical correlation between the phases of the moon at a particular time of year and the production of truffles. On the other hand, they also say that this cannot be extrapolated to cover the period during which new truffle-grounds are planted out, since the moon may well have an influence in this case.

Even if its effects cannot be measured exactly, the influence of the moon cannot be denied, as it has always affected the growth of plants as it has the tides. Truffle-growers are probably more sensitive to this belief, since they have very little control over the development of their crop, and might thus resort to superstition to explain the mysterious development of the truffle underground.

Musky Truffle

Tuber brumale, the musky or black winter truffle, is called *ivernenco* in Provence. It never grows larger than an egg. It looks like the black truffle* (*Tuber melanosporum*), but when studied closely it reveals several differences. The warty peridium is blackish and very rough and never reddens prior to maturity. The gleba is grayish-black on maturity and shot through with thick white veins that are widely spaced and do not turn red when cut. The musky truffle is harvested from November through March in the same areas of production as *T. melanosporum*. It has a grassy aroma, reminiscent of damp soil and undergrowth, that cannot be compared with that of the black truffle. It tastes slightly bitter, with a musky note, but when cooked it is quite tasty with eggs—in an omelet for instance. It is often used in cooked meats that are labeled "truffled." In the natural ecosystem, this truffle competes strongly with *T. melanosporum*. It is less demanding as to soil and climate, so that its mycorrhiza* are far more invasive and will often supplant the black truffle, even in cultivated truffle-grounds. It is thus the enemy of truffle-growers who are trying to find a way of stopping it from contaminating their plantations. Research on truffle-bearing trees shows that the hazel is particularly prone to being invaded by the musky truffle in preference to the true black truffle. Consumers are also wary of it, since they risk paying the high price of the Périgord truffle only to be sold this inferior species. It is very difficult to identify it in the markets, especially when it is sold covered in soil inside burlap bags or secreted at the bottom of a basket. By discreetly digging a nail into the peridium, it can be ascertained that the skin is softer, and its scales are smaller than those of the black truffle, and fall off when brushed. *T. brumale* is harvested in southwestern and southeastern France, in Spain, and in Italy.

Late fourteenth-century ink drawing attributed to Baldini. Bibliothèque nationale de France, Paris.

■ Mycelium

The mycelium is the result of the germination, in spring, of the spores* produced by the fruiting bodies (truffles). It has the appearance of a network of branching filaments that spread through the soil. These filaments, known as hyphae, are only three to five microns in diameter in the truffle and are therefore invisible to the naked eye. Hyphae can be seen under the microscope on the surface of certain mycorrhiza. They are straw-colored or reddish.

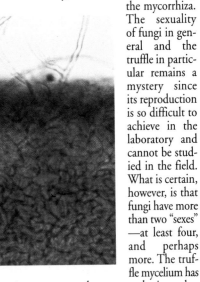

Fungi of the genus *Tuber**, like all hypogeous (underground) fungi, live in a symbiotic association with green plants. The fungus mycelium infects the young roots of certain species of host tree for which it shows a preference. It produces mycorrhiza*—tiny clubs of barely measurable length, whose color varies from brown to orange and which have important and very specialized functions. This process is called "mycorrhization." The mycelium is propagated under climatic conditions

Mycelium of *Tuber melanosporum* on the mycorrhiza.

that have still not been fully determined, probably in spring or fall. The filaments of the mycelium (carrying the fruiting-body) that produced the mycorrhiza continue to spread and ramify, invading the soil and ensuring fruiting as well as nutrition in the initial stage of truffle formation. How this process works is still a matter for conjecture. The fruiting-body begins to grow as the result of the fusion of filaments of complementary sexual polarity, most of which are issued by the mycorrhiza. The sexuality of fungi in general and the truffle in particular remains a mystery since its reproduction is so difficult to achieve in the laboratory and cannot be studied in the field. What is certain, however, is that fungi have more than two "sexes" —at least four, and perhaps more. The truffle mycelium has a tendency to colonize other growing roots and itself grows by about a foot each year, which explains how the area of production shifts from year to year. As it exhausts the nutritional substances in the soil, the mycelium tends to act as a herbicide, causing the carpet of greenery at the foot of the tree to disappear. This is the area known as the burnt patch*, which is a good indication of the presence of truffles or a sign that a young tree will soon begin producing them.

◼ Mycorrhiza

"Mycorrhiza" is a portmanteau word that combines *myco* meaning "fungus" and *rhiza* meaning "root." It is the hybrid that results from an association between the mycelium* of the fungus and the roots of the truffle-bearing tree. This association, known as symbiosis, occurs in nature, but in the case of the cultivated truffle it has been induced artificially by creating the link between the fungus and the tree. This is achieved by inoculating seedlings or saplings with mycelium. The fungus (truffle) mycelium reaches the tiny side-roots of the tree, infects them, and forms mycorrhiza, tiny club-shaped excrescences of barely measurable length that, in the case of the black truffle*, are brown or orange in color. The mycorrhiza has several functions. First of all, it protects the mycelium during winter and helps it to propagate during warm weather, but its other main purpose is to exchange nutrients between the mycelium, the tree, and the soil. There are as many types of mycorrhiza as there are symbiotic fungi, so they are hard to identify in the absence of the fruiting-body. For this reason, inferior species of truffle and other fungi can easily invade the truffle-ground*. In the case of the hazel tree, for example, especially where it is under mechanical cultivation, mycorrhization frequently occurs with *Tuber brumale* at the expense of *Tuber melanosporum*. The truffle-grower has to combat the invasions of unwanted species such as *T. brumale* and *Tuber aestivum*, which, under natural conditions, would flourish alongside their more sought-after rival in equal numbers.

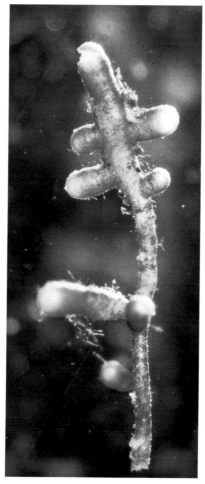

Side-roots infected by the mycorrhiza of *Tuber melanosporum.*

Identifying a species by smell.

■ NOSE

"My nose, quoth the poet, hiding a tear,
So grotesque in Paris, has charm in Dordogne:
For sniffing out truffles and Monbazillac."

Edmond Rostand, *Cyrano de Bergerac*

A magazine dedicated to edible fungus organized a blind tasting of different types of truffle for six wine specialists who were unfamiliar with truffles. The black truffle* was described as being "a country smell that was nevertheless subtle, powerful, and intense, that was simultaneously cool and 'hot,' and that had an extraordinary persistence. The notes alternated between animal and vegetable and included newly-cut or dried grass, moist tobacco, decaying oak-leaves, roots, humus, damp earth, leaf-mold, dried mushrooms especially the horn of plenty, as well as musk, damp leather, fox fur, and lightly smoked cured meats. Some of the smells had sexual connotations, though others noted a sweeter note of ripe stone-fruits."

The white truffle* was considered to be "strong, powerful, spicy, piquant, peppery and sulfurous, with its well-known note of methane gas. It is redolent of cabbage, as well as raw garlic, onion, chives, green onion, nettle, water in which leeks have been cooked, vegetables of the fennel type, with aniseed and even minty notes. Unlike the other truffles, there is nothing about its fragrance to associate it with dried fungi. In the mouth, the white truffle is delicate, sweet, and more buttery than the others. The flavors are powerful, with a very persistent aroma, very long in the mouth. After the initial piquant, spicy attack, the flavors of cabbage, garlic, celery, and cheese appear, subsequently mellowing into hazelnut and walnut. The finale reverts to being more peppery with the buttery quality of a strong cheese of the parmesan type."

■ Oak (pubescent)

The pubescent oak is the type most likely to bear truffles. For several thousand years, northern Europe was covered in forests of hornbeam, beech, and oak. Some localities even feature the oak in their heraldic insignia, showing how important the tree was to them. For instance, the coat of arms of Richerenches* in southern France, well known for its truffle market, contains an oak tree. Since the yields of the natural truffle-grounds* had been diminishing significantly since 1870, truffle-growers planted, under supervision, the most suitable species of oak for their region, infected with the mycorrhiza of *Tuber melanosporum*. The pubescent white oak, so called because of the downy underside of the leaves, does not shed its leaves in winter, and is able to cope very well with the aridity of the limestone plateaux and aerated soil typical of the Mediterranean basin. It is the black truffle's

Pubescent oak.

A truffle-bearing tree, identifiable by the presence of the burnt patch.

best friend, though it takes between ten and fifteen years before the first truffles can be harvested. The holm-oak or evergreen oak, on the other hand, which is able to cope with stony soil and drought, will start producing truffles after six or seven years. Connoisseurs maintain that truffles grown under oak trees are more fragrant, a claim that is also made for ceps (*porcini*). The oak tree is a tree sacred to every tradition. The truffle that develops on its roots was considered for centuries to be a gift from the gods. The Celts, whose beliefs persisted into the Middle Ages, considered the tree to be a reflection of the axis of the world, the relationship between heaven and earth. According to them, the oak attracted lightning bolts, and these created the truffle, believed to be an accretion of earth formed where the lightning struck the ground.

Parasites and Pests

When truffle cultivators plant mycorrhized saplings that they have acquired from agricultural research institutes, they assume they will be harvesting the black truffle*, *Tuber melanosporum*. But it's not that simple. There are other species of truffle that can supersede the black truffle. At present, researchers and agronomists are actively trying to combat the invasion of cultivated truffle-grounds by *Tuber brumale*, the musky truffle*, which is an inferior species. At a recent seminar, an Italian scientist showed how much easier it is to inoculate a young tree with *T. brumale* than with *T. melanosporum*. If one gram of fresh black truffle is needed to inoculate a single sapling with the mycorrhiza*, it is possible to inoculate 10,000 seedlings with the same quantity of *T. brumale*! As for the reason why, in addition to the scientific explanations,

T.brumale is much hardier and mycorrhizes more easily than *T. melanosporum*. It is particularly invasive in wet springs and falls, when there is a drop in pH in the soil and where the soil is too compacted. However, a balance tends to develop between the two species. *T. melanosporum* appears to grow particularly well in the company of vines and lavender, although it does not form mycorrhiza with either of these plants. The Italian white truffle*, *Tuber magnatum*, seems to be less sensitive than *T. melanosporum* to competition from mycorrhiza of other species. Hazelnut saplings are more easily contaminated by *T. brumale*, and they could be used as a "marker" to test the presence of this species in the soil, before planting out a truffle-ground*. Recent work also shows that *Tuber aestivum*, the summer truffle*, is even more invasive than *T. brumale*, but the latter continues to be the main target of the truffle-growers who want to eradicate it.

Tuber brumale, the musky truffle.

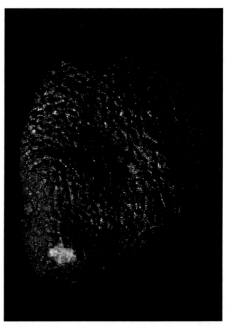

67

Preceding double page: Sorges-en-Périgord, France.

■ Périgord and Quercy

Périgord is the south-western region of France that includes the Dordogne, Quercy, Lot, and part of the département of Tarn-et-Garonne. The landscape generally consists of the high, arid limestone plateaux typical of the Mediterranean basin, which are covered in truffle-bearing oaks* (pubescent oaks). The stony, arid landscape is dotted with villages with white or pale yellow houses and dovecotes. These are villages whose names mean much to the truffle-lover: Sarlat, Saint-Alvère, Brantôme, and Sorges-en-Périgord. In Quercy, there are Lalbenque, Limogne-en-Quercy, Cahors, Martel, Gramat, and, further south, Caussade. Each holds a weekly market* during the truffle season*. The black truffle* that is valued for its fragrance and eating quality is most frequently known outside France as the Périgord truffle, although it is found elsewhere in southwest France. It is harvested in the southwest (Périgord and Quercy) and the southeast of France (Vaucluse, Var, Drôme and Gard), and in Spain and Italy. There is little difference

between European black truffles of the *Tuber melanosporum* species, but whether the black truffles grown outside Europe are of equal eating quality remains to be seen. The name "Périgord" is not, in this case, an indication of origin, because the black truffle has been known under this name since the nineteenth century, and restaurants serve black truffles under the name "Périgord truffles," irrespective of where they were grown.

The little village of Sorges in Périgord was famous for its truffles in the early twentieth century. Here, a team consisting of an ethnologist, an agronomist, a historian, and a sociologist have founded an ecological museum dedicated to the truffle, covering every aspect of its history, cultivation, and gastronomic properties. There are extensive displays and a great deal of documentation (rare books, press cuttings, and the works of 700 authors from Pliny the Younger to present-day writers). A path then leads through the truffle-beds, a nursery of truffle-bearing trees about a mile long, illustrating the work of the truffle-grower.

Landscape in Quercy.

71

■ PIG

Truffle-hunting* using a pig is traditional in many truffle-growing regions, from France to China. The first pigs were let into European truffle-grounds in the mid-sixteenth century. The sow, who is better-tempered and easier to handle than the hog, soon proved herself to be much more talented than either the hog or the gilt at finding the delicacy. Truffle-hunters long used a breed descended from Spanish black pigs, particularly talented at hunting out truffles. The purebred sow has disappeared owing to multiple crossings with other breeds, but her descendants have retained the qualities that are indispensable for truffle-hunting, namely a certain preference for long hikes, a lively disposition, and, most importantly, an extremely well-developed sense of smell as well as a marked interest in truffles (unlike the truffle-hound*, the pig hunts truffles purely for its personal gratification). It is easy to train a pig to hunt truffles and should not take more than three weeks. As far as breeders are concerned, a "good" piglet is the most lively of the litter and the one that rushes over when a handful of truffles is held out to it. Once the piglet has been won over it needs to learn to appreciate in equal measure the other delicacies (grains of corn, a piece of bread, a slice of cooked potato, etc.) with which it will be rewarded when it has unearthed a truffle. The training process begins in a corner of the farmyard, where the pig learns to find a truffle. Then comes the time to assess how partial it is to truffles, and whether it is fond enough of the fungus to dig for it in the wild. The pig does best in truffle-grounds that are

easily accessible and where the gradient is not too steep. It sniffs and snuffles, digs in the earth with its snout, and finally unearths the prize. The owner needs to have quick reactions and to be strong—a pig can weigh as much as 220 pounds—to be able to

quickly remove the tuber from the animal before it gets a chance to eat it. Sometimes a small wooden wedge needs to be slipped into the pig's mouth to force it to let go of its find, but once it has been rewarded, it is happy to continue the quest.

Truffle-hunting on the Plateau of Valensole.

73

The egg and the truffle, perfect companions.

■ Preserving

If the truffle is bought for private consumption, there are several ways of preserving it. If it is to be eaten in the few days following purchase, wrap the truffle, without brushing off the dirt, in absorbent paper and store it in the refrigerator. One classic way of using it is to put it in a sealed jar with eggs which will then become saturated with the truffle fragrance. A fresh truffle left in the refrigerator will impregnate all other foodstuffs with its smell.

If the truffle is not going to be eaten straight away, it can be stored in the freezer, where it will keep for nine to twelve months. To freeze a truffle, wash it and brush it lightly, then dry with a soft cloth. It can also be frozen in oil. Place it in a small glass jar, cover it completely with a flavorless vegetable oil, such as corn or grapeseed oil (or you could use goose fat), and seal the jar. The truffle can also be wrapped in foil, placed in a small glass jar, and hermetically sealed before freezing. When

defrosted, the truffle will recover most of its aromatic qualities but not its texture, as freezing softens it. It is thus preferable to grate the truffle as soon as it comes out of the freezer, while it is still frozen. The flavored oil can be used in salads.

If the truffle is for commercial use, canning is mainly carried out by professional bottlers and canners*, but it can also be done by individuals. Truffles can be preserved in cans, with the addition of a little water and salt, provided professional canning equipment is used (sometimes a professional canner will seal your cans for you). They can also be bottled in Mason jars. The truffles must first be sterilized by boiling them to a temperature of just above 100°C (212°F) for at least one hour. This process causes the truffles to lose some of their fragrance and around twenty per cent of their weight. The truffle juice is preserved for use in omelettes. Truffles preserved in this way can be kept for three years in a cool, dry place.

■ PRICES

"[...] It is the most capricious, the most revered of black princesses. It costs its weight in gold ..."

Prisons and Paradise, Colette.

Truffle prices vary according to supply and demand. The fresh black truffle (*Tuber melanosporum*), of which France is the main consumer, fetches quite high prices in the markets, because demand exceeds supply and truffle growth depends on the vagaries of nature, the season* and the time of year. Naturally, prices rise during the holidays and at the end of the season when they are scarcer, but of better quality, having had plenty of time to ripen. The prices indicated below are approximate, though fairly realistic, and their relative value has remained unchanged for a century. Burgundy truffles are cheaper at the beginning of the season, when they are of lesser quality. Prices for the Périgord or black truffle*, and even for the musky truffle* (*Tuber brumale*) can start at US$48 per pound at the beginning of the season and reach up to $120 or $180 per pound by the end. Spain usually has lower prices at the beginning and end of the season, unless France, its biggest customer, is having a bad year. Italy has even greater difficulty managing its production and harvesting, but in the year 2000 the black truffle cost around $155–200 per pound and the white truffle* (*Tuber magnatum Pico*) reached between $900 and $1,195 per pound. The Burgundy truffle* (*Tuber uncinatum*), which is only sold brushed and washed, fetched an average of $90 a pound and the summer truffle* (*Tuber aestivum*) $36–42 per pound. As for the Chinese truffle* (*Tuber indicum*) it barely managed $21 per pound.

The price of a truffle in a gourmet store or bought from a dealer will be double the market price. And yet, despite its high value, the truffle does not make its growers rich. Very few of them can afford to live from truffle-growing, as the yield is so small.

■ PRODUCING COUNTRIES

France is the greatest consumer of truffles and officially produces somewhere in the region of twenty to forty metric tons of black truffles* (*Tuber melanosporum*) annually.

Production is divided between two regions—the southwest, including the départements of Lot and Dordogne, and the southeast, mainly the départements of Vaucluse, Var, Drôme, and Gard. Most truffles are produced in the southeast, the area roughly covered by Provence. Burgundy (as well as the neighboring regions of Champagne, Lorraine, and Franche-Comté) are doing what they can to foster the production of the Burgundy truffle* (*Tuber uncinatum*), which is as tasty as the black truffle but has long been neglected.

In Spain, the black truffle grows in the northeast, along with the musky truffle* (*Tuber brumale*) and the summer truffle* (*Tuber aestivum*). It is found in Catalonia, Valencia, Teruel, Cuenca, Guadalajara, Huesca, and Saragossa, and a small amount is produced further south, in the Valencia and Seville areas. Most of these truffles are exported to France where they are sold wholesale, retailed domestically, or re-exported. There is not much demand for truffles in Spain, either from individuals or from the food industry, even in restaurants. Only in Madrid has interest in the product been aroused. There are large wholesale markets* there at which as many truffles are sold as in France.

Italy, like France, has a strong truffle-growing and truffle-eating tradition. Alba* in Piedmont is the home of the white truffle* (*Tuber magnatum Pico*), where it has a place of honor, but the

1. Catalonia
2. Aragon
3. Castille-La Manc
4. Valencia

Production areas in Europe for
Tuber melanosporum and *Tuber magnatum*.

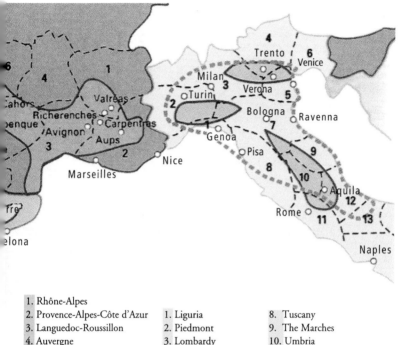

1. Rhône-Alpes	1. Liguria	8. Tuscany
2. Provence-Alpes-Côte d'Azur	2. Piedmont	9. The Marches
3. Languedoc-Roussillon	3. Lombardy	10. Umbria
4. Auvergne	4. Trentino	11. Latium
5. Midi-Pyrénées	5. Veneto	12. The Abruzzi
6. Limousin	6. Friuli	13. Molise
7. Poitou-Charentes	7. Emilia Romagna	14. Campagna
8. Aquitaine		

white and black truffles are also found in Liguria, Lombardy, Trentino, Veneto, Emilia Romagna, Tuscany, the Marches, and the Abruzzi. Molise is the largest producer of the white truffle, and Umbria produces both white and black truffles. Latium, Campania, Basilicata, Sicily, and most recently Sardinia, have a small production of *T. melanosporum*. Italy is the only country to produce *T. magnatum Pico* (if one discounts a few acres in Slovenia and Croatia).

Apart from the three big European producers, Slovenia and Croatia grow both black and white truffles, and Germany and Poland have the inferior musky truffle. The Oregon white truffle grows in Oregon and Washington in the United States, and there have reportedly been successful attempts at planting the black truffle. New Zealand has recently tried its hand at cultivating *T. melanosporum* and *T. magnatum*. The first black truffles grown in Tasmania were dug up in 2000, and black truffles have even been harvested in Israel. Finally, China mainly produces the inferior Chinese truffle* (*Tuber indicum*), principally for home consumption, but Western producers are worried that the expanding Chinese export market could undercut their prices, with inferior truffles being sold fraudulently as top-quality produce.

Recipes with Truffles

Foie gras and truffles is one of those classic combinations, once tasted, never forgotten. The town of Strasbourg is the birthplace of truffled foie gras.

In the eighteenth century, the Maréchal de Contades asked his cook, Jean-Pierre Clauses, to produce an exceptional dish for him. This turned out to be a pâté de foie gras *en croûte* (in

Boelemma
de Stomme
Maerten, *The
Truffled Pie.*
Oil on wood.
Musée des
Beaux-Arts,
Nantes, France.

pastry). At a later date, a chef named Nicolas Doyen left his native Périgord for Strasbourg, where he improved upon this foie gras dish by adding truffles from his native region. The truffled foie gras was an immediate success, being even more popular than the foie gras dish created by Clauses, and Strasbourg pâté earned international renown. These pâtés then

79

found their way back to Périgord. The aristocracy and the well-to-do developed a passion for the dish, and it became fashionable to present it as a gift in elaborate china terrines decorated and painted by famous artists. Another dish, the pâté de Périgueux, then gained popularity. This consisted of layers of foie gras, pâté and truffles, packed into cans. The combination of foie gras and the truffle was now firmly established.

Turkey and chicken were also often roasted with slices of truffle inserted between the skin and flesh, and nestling on beds of whole truffles—a recipe known as " half in mourning " (*demi-deuil*) because of the color of the truffles against the white flesh of the bird. The composer, Rossini, an accomplished cook, created a famous salad of Italian white truffles. Curnonsky, a famous gourmet, claimed that "the truffle is to foie gras what the pearl is to its setting." If the truffle was used profusely and carelessly at that time, thanks to much greater production, today legislation controls the sale of products that are entitled to call themselves "truffled" (what percentage of truffle must be included, what species are acceptable, and so on).

■ Religion

For centuries, the Church fiercely rejected the truffle as being far too black to merit being called divine. Consequently, in truffling centers such as Valréas, Saint-Paul-Trois-Châteaux, and Richerenches in southeastern France, and in Lalbenque in the southwest, prayers are offered up to Saint Anthony*, the patron saint of truffle-gatherers, in the hope of a good harvest. The most famous of these

masses is held at Richerenches, a former command post of the Knights Templar. This little village in Provence is famous for the black truffle*, *Tuber melanosporum*, and is the home of the largest truffle market* in Europe, where transactions are conducted with the utmost discretion. In 1952, the parish priest of Richerenches had the idea of celebrating a special Mass devoted to truffles, which were the source of the village's prosperity. Ever since, the ceremony has been held under the patronage of Saint Anthony. The Mass is held on the third Sunday in January, close to Saint Anthony's feast day.

As the day dawns, the faithful deposit truffles in baskets in the church as offerings—an act of reconciliation, since the Church had traditionally considered the finding of a truffle a mere matter of luck and not to be the fruit of any labor. The donation of truffles harks back to an old harvest tradition—the "offering"—when shepherds, peasants, and fishermen offer what they had produced or harvested. "Good Saint Anthony," the locals pray, "may you grant truffles in abundance, and may their odor and pleasant flavor make Provence beloved of all." The resulting collection of truffles is weighed in the concourse in front of the church and sold by auction.

■ Richerenches

Richerenches was a favorite retreat of the popes of Avignon and a former stronghold of the Knights Templar. The village has the best-preserved Knights Templar command post in Provence, and it was recently classified as a national heritage site. From November through mid-March, the largest truffle market* in France—and indeed in the world—is held at Richerenches on Saturday mornings. This market alone trades thirty percent of the total French production. The market is held in the village street lined with magnificent plane trees, whose branches are bare at that time of year. It is an informal and festive affair. Starting at 9:30 a.m., a few truffle-hunters arrive and loiter in the street with their truffles in a sack, offering to show their wares to anyone who wishes to see them. Would-be purchasers can go are conducted quietly and privately, by gentlemen's agreement and in cash, and the truffles are weighed on old-fashioned scales. As the street fills with the fragrance of truffles, the crowd begins to arrive and swells until midday, although by that time there is little hope of buying a truffle. In the local café, the truffle-gatherers congregate to drink a well-deserved kir, while the truffle-lovers await a fragrantly truffled omelet. There is much talk of the black truffle*, that magic fungus which stirs up great passion in locals and visitors alike. It is

from one to the other to examine, smell, and touch them, and to question the owners. The brokers arrive a little later. They gather around the trunks of the parked cars along the road that runs through the village, haggling over prices. The truffle-growers seek out the brokers, whom they have known for most of their lives. Negotiations also honored for its role in regenerating the countryside after the phylloxera plague which attacked vines in the late nineteenth century.

In late January, the famous Truffle Mass is held at Richerenches. The collection takes the form of truffles, which are donated to the parish for the upkeep of the church.

Sant ANTONIO ABATE

■ SAINT ANTHONY

Saint Anthony is the patron saint of truffle-growers. If one considers the symbols of the iconography of Saint Anthony, his connection with the truffle is quickly apparent. At the age of twenty-five, Saint Anthony retreated into the Theban desert to live as an ascetic. He is depicted wearing a tau-cross on his shoulder and a halo around his head. He carries a long staff. Saint Anthony founded numerous monasteries of the Antonine order. The monks flourished in France, in particular during the eleventh century. Although Saint Anthony's way of life required him to resist temptation, he no doubt tasted the *terfez**, the desert truffle that is harvested with a staff. The Antonine monks were hospitaliers, and were known to cure "Saint Anthony's fire" or ergotism, the result of accidentally ingesting a fungus called *Claviceps purpurea* or ergot that grows on grain, mainly rye. The monks recommended pork fat as a remedy. Their pigs had a tau-cross branded on their ear and wore bells, giving them the right to roam the streets and feed on garbage. In the Christian tradition, the pig is impure, uninhibited, lubricious, and destructive, while the wild boar is considered demonic. Among the Celts, however, the wild boar was a symbol of spiritual authority and knowledge. This could well have led the wild boar to be associated with a skill at unearthing truffles, considered to be the mysterious products of lightning. The animal's appetite for acorns, the fruit of the sacred oak, further caused it to be venerated. In the iconography of Saint Anthony, however, an association with the pig or wild boar does not emerge until the fourteenth century; it was not until the sixteenth century that the Church gave its blessing to the truffle, which was by then being served at the tables of kings. The pig, whose help was needed for unearthing the truffles, was then placed under the protection of the saint, whose image became associated with truffle-harvesting. The healing pig thus became the truffle-hunting pig.

■ Seasons

The black truffle* season begins from late October to late November, and ends in March. The truffles start the season with the reddish peridium of truffles that are not yet ripe, and the gleba is white. It is not until early January that truffles can be bought whose peridium is black and whose gleba is chocolate brown marbled with white veins. It takes a few light frosts for them to ripen. Only then will they have the powerful, heady perfume that indicates that truffle is absolutely ripe. It is best to wait until mid-January for a truffle to be at its best and most fragrant. Unfortunately, January is also the month most to be feared because the weather is at its worst. Truffles are like fruit, in that they suffer if there are more than ten degrees of frost. Below this temperature, the truffle freezes, turns into water and loses all of its flavor and odor.

Saint Anthony, patron of truffle-growers.

Truffle-ground in the snow.

In Italy, the season begins in September and ends in late December for both the black and the white truffle*. The summer truffle* or St John's truffle (*Tuber aestivum*) is picked from May through September. Most producing countries regulate the dates of harvesting in order to preserve the truffle-bearing trees from the worst rigors of the climate. This is

also a way of preventing poaching of "marked truffles", which can be detected in August by small swellings on the surface of the soil. This control enables the last truffles at the end of the season to remain in the soil and release their spores*, which, in association with the mycelium*, regenerates the fungus and helps it to fruit more abundantly the following year.

The best soil for truffle production has certain special characteristics. A truffle breathes; it inhales oxygen and exhales carbon dioxide. It does particularly well in thin soil over a limestone substrate that is easily warmed by the sun and that hosts intense biological activity. The soil in which the truffle grows is shallow, since the truffle develops from four to twelve inches below the surface, and consists mainly of limestone with traces of other minerals, especially clay. Limestone is indispensable for its lightness, brittle texture and porosity. A small amount of clay helps to regulate the humidity of the soil and only becomes an

insects and earthworms underground and by the presence of organic matter on which the truffle is able to feed. In an artificial truffle-ground*, correct preparation of the soil is vital for the development of the side-roots of the truffle-bearing oak*. The soil also needs to be worked and well aerated a few months prior to planting the trees, as soon as the first rains of the Mediterranean season begin (in the fall), rendering the earth malleable. The soil thus remains longer in contact with the atmospheric agents. The perfect subsoil for truffle-beds is a base of hard, compact rocks that promote the growth of surface side-roots and root-hairs. Natural fissures in the rock enable excess water to drain away quickly and prevent the formation underground of stagnant pools that could inhibit the growth of the mycelium*.

obstacle if it is present in concentrations of more than forty-five percent. Even though a truffle needs water, it cannot tolerate excessive humidity. The ability of the soil to drain water but retain it at a greater depth also helps to mitigate the effects of summer drought. Aeration of the soil is achieved mainly by the activity of

Section through the soil and subsoil of a truffle-bed.

A truffle plantation in Navarre, Spain.

■ Spain

Spanish truffles come exclusively from uncultivated truffle-grounds. Spain is not known for its consumption of truffles, although interest has increased in the last few years in the major cities of Madrid and Barcelona. Spain therefore exports eighty percent of what it produces to France, where the truffles are processed and preserved. Spain boasts the largest truffle-ground* in the world, near Soria, on a plateau located around 130 miles from Madrid. It covers an area of 1500 acres. The owner is Salvador Arotz, a magnate in the food industry, who has a passion for mushrooms and truffles. The woodland is surrounded by a few small fields of wheat, sabines—a variety of juniper also found in the southern U.S.—and Scots pines. Most of the host trees are evergreen oak, a species well suited to this environment. Its roots are slow-growing, which has the advantage of inhibiting the invasion of undesirable hypogeous fungi, such as the musky truffle*, yet black truffles* are produced at quite an early stage

in the life of the tree. Pubescent, or truffle-bearing oaks*, and a few hazel trees also grow on the truffle-ground. All these trees produce their valuable crop naturally, since the technique of inoculation with mycorrhiza* did not exist at the time when they were planted. A nursery has now been established, however, in which saplings are inoculated with black truffle spores* in order to obtain a mycorrhized plant. The saplings are reared in an indoor environment and are watered with the same frequency as they would be in the wild, with the aid of a rolling spray mechanism of the type used in cornfields. The height of trees is kept low. The proportions of truffles produced are ninety percent black truffle* (*Tuber melanosporum*), nine percent summer truffle* (*Tuber aestivum*) and one percent fall truffle* (*Tuber brumale*) and other species, but the actual quantities remain a secret. This truffle-growing experiment may not be in the ecological spirit of truffle-growing in the wild—but it will no doubt make a valuable contribution to research.

■ SPECIES OF TRUFFLE

Truffles are first classified by genus (for instance, *Tuber*, the Latin word for excrescence), then by species (*magnatum*, for example), and finally (in some cases) by the name of the mycologist who first identified the species (for instance, Pico, in the case of the white truffle). Truffles are classed in species, not varieties. In Europe, nine species of *Tuber* are generally sold commercially. They grow in winter, summer, and fall, depending on the species. It is very hard for an amateur or novice to be able to recognize the differences in the peridium (skin) and gleba (flesh) of the various kinds of truffle or to distinguish the various aromas, but the following list gives the consumer an indication of the diversity and specific characteristics of each truffle.

Tuber melanosporum is known variously as the black truffle*, the Périgord truffle, the Tricastin truffle, or the Norcia truffle. *Tuber brumale*, the musky truffle*, is a fall truffle of inferior quality. *Tuber indicum*, the Chinese truffle*, has exactly the same growing season as the prized black truffle. It is a variety of little value. *Tuber uncinatum*, the Burgundy truffle*, is closely related to the black truffle and also grows in winter. *Tuber mesentericum*, a related variety, is of little culinary interest.

As for the white truffles*, *Tuber magnatum*, the white Piedmont or Alba truffle, is a fall species, as is *Tuber macrosporum*, but another white species, *Tuber borchii*, known as the March white truffle and almost exclusively confined to Italy, is found in spring, summer and fall.

Tuber aestivum is known as the summer truffle* or St John's truffle (St John's day is Midsummer Day) to reflect its time of ripening. This truffle is also to be found in northern Europe, and at one time it was hunted with dogs in Hampshire, England.

Italian white truffles are sold in most countries, but Spain does not permit the sale of inferior white truffles, although it allows the sale of *T. magnatum* and of black truffles of no culinary interest, such as *T. brumale*. *T. melanosporum* sales are permitted of course, but the summer truffle, *T. aestivum* cannot be imported or exported. The United States has its own truffle species, including *Tuber gibbosum*, the Oregon white truffle, *Tuber texense*, the Texas truffle, and *Tuber canaliculatum*, which is found in the northern United States and southern Canada. A recently discovered truffle, *Tuber himalayense*, grows in the mountainous regions of Asia. This may be a new species or may simply be *T. indicum*. The eastern Mediterranean produces an underground fungus known as the *terfez*, desert, or sand truffle, which belongs to a different genus, that of Terfezia. It was highly prized by the Romans and may yet come back into fashion.

The truffle-hunter is likely to encounter other subterranean fungi that vary from country to country, such as *Tuber rufum* or the dog-nose truffle, a small, smooth-skinned truffle whose flesh is orange colored, and *Tuber excavatum*, a yellow-ocher, flattish fungus that smells of celery root but is not edible.

White Piedmont truffle and Perigord truffle, in G. Bresadola, *Funghi mangerecci et venenosi*, vol. II, pl. 223.

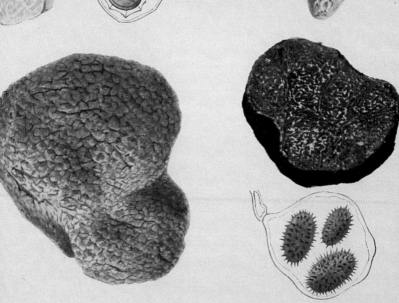

1 *Tuber magnatum Pico*
2 *Tuber melanosporum Vitt.*

et O. Mattirolo del.

■ Spore

A spore is a single-celled organism from which a fungus reproduces. In the case of fungi whose reproduction is sexual, as in the family of Ascomycetes (to which the truffle belongs), the spores are formed on asci or sacs. They vary in number, but one ascus will contain up to eight spores. The asci release their spores as the fruiting-body decays. Spore dissemination in the case of hypogeous fungi, such as the truffle (*Tuber*), is carried out by insects, earthworms, and small mammals. A fungus like the truffle, whose whole life cycle takes place underground, has fewer opportunities for dispersing its spores than a fungus whose spores are produced above ground, as in the case of the mushroom or the morel (another Ascomycete). When the disseminated spores germinate, they produce the mycelium*, which, in the case of the truffle, infects the roots of the truffle-bearing tree and creates mycorrhiza*. If a food product claims to contain truffles and examination under the microscope reveals spores that are echinulate (covered in short, stiff hairs) the truffle in question is likely to be the black truffle* or the musky truffle*. If the spores are alveolate (honey-combed) they are likely to be the spores of the summer truffle*. Examination of the spores is by far the surest way of identifying a species of truffle. The white veins of the gleba (the truffle flesh) are sterile, but the darker areas are where the

Tuber brumale spores.

spore-sacs form. The spores and their sacs darken upon maturity, producing the black pigmentation that is characteristic of the black truffle*.

■ Sterilization

In 1790, the Frenchman Nicolas Appert found a new way of preserving fresh produce by canning, a process that is still known as "appertization." It was discovered that sterilization—the action of destroying toxins through heating—could preserve food for several years. Prior to this, the only ways in which foods could be preserved was by submerging them in grease, oil, vinegar or alcohol. Mason jars and home-canning apparatus can be used at home, but industrial canners sterilize foods in an autoclave.

The procedure for preserving* is as follows. Truffles are brushed and washed, and may or may not be peeled. They are then packed into large cans with a little water to hydrate them and a little salt. The addition of wine, liqueur, or brandy is optional. The cans are then heated in a water-bath which must boil at 230 to 248°F (110 to 120°C), for ninety minutes to two hours. During this process, the truffles lose between fifteen and twenty-five percent of their weight. The cooking liquid produced by the truffles (truffle juice) is then drained off and used for other purposes, and the truffles are then boiled again in small cans for individual consumption. At this point the truffle should reach the net weight stated on the can. Unfortunately, the second boiling deprives the truffle of most of its aroma, and any residual fragrance will disappear completely two hours after the can has been opened. That is why the top chefs always buy truffles from the first boiling. Truffle juice is also sold sterilized, as well as a range of truffle products for every taste. There are peeled or unpeeled truffles that have merely been brushed; round, uniformly shaped truffles; less regularly shaped truffles; truffle pieces; truffle shavings and truffle morsels. About twenty canners process tons of truffles in France, Spain, and Italy.

Summer Truffle

Only one species of truffle is harvested in the summer in Europe. The summer truffle* (*Tuber aestivum*) is also known as St John's truffle because St John's Day is Midsummer Day. It looks like the Périgord truffle but is often larger. It is also closely related to the Burgundy truffle* (*Tuber uncinatum*), whose fragrance is stronger. It is not liked by canners, and its only advantages are that it is the only truffle available during the summer, and that its price is modest, at around $30 per pound. The peridium is covered in prominent scales, and the gleba is pale and veined with white, which has earned it the name of white truffle, although the flesh turns beige when ripe. It is a different species from *Tuber magnatum*, the white Alba or Piedmont truffle, which is strongly scented and remains white inside and out. The summer truffle has a faint odor of mushrooms, undergrowth, and roasted barley malt, and it tastes of hazelnuts. The French consider it to be of little culinary value, although some cooks are able to make it taste good raw or added to hot dishes at the last moment, since its aromas are very volatile. Its white flesh has tempted some to darken it artificially, and it has also been sold as the "Périgord white truffle." It grows all over Europe, from Spain, Italy, and France to Germany and southern England. It was once hunted with dogs in Hampshire, England, though it was never traded commercially there. The summer truffle lives in symbiosis with oak, pine, beech, hazel, and hornbeam, in calcareous soil. In France, where it is traded, production amounts to ten to fifteen metric tons a year. It is harvested from May through the end of September.

Tuber aestivum.

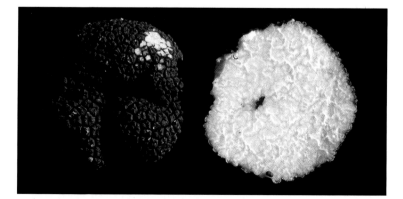

Terfez

The white desert truffle was famous long before the black truffle*, which only came to prominence in the eighteenth century. The *terfez* had a great reputation in antiquity. It was believed to be the product of lightning and divine intervention. The truffle of antiquity has clearly been identified as the desert truffle, or *terfez*, which is also highly praised in Arab literature. The *terfez* of the Libyan desert, also found in North Africa and the Sinai Peninsula, is an underground fungus of the genus *Terfezia*, whose botanical characteristics are different from those of *Tuber*. It is approximately the same size as the black truffle, but matures in spring. The flavor is said to be the same as that of St George's mushroom (*Calocybe gambosum*), and it has little fragrance. Traces of it have been found in Mesopotamia, where the Sumerians prized it. At a later date, the Roman emperors brought it from Libya (when it was known as the white truffle of Cyrenaica), being totally unaware that they had their own native white truffle*. *Terfez* specimens were packed in sealed jars and preserved in sand, honey, or vinegar. It was a luxury item, a gourmet product used in spicy sauces flavored with cinnamon, ginger, and *garum*, the salty fish-sauce without which no Roman dish was complete. Apicius gives a recipe for roasting truffles then lightly coating them with sauce. The *terfez* is still popular in North Africa and Iran, and it is used in traditional Jewish cooking from that part of the world, flavored with a spice mixture called *ras-el-hanout* that contains twelve spices, but is mostly composed of coriander seed. The fungus itself has little flavor, but the spices make it tasty, and the recipes have wonderful names, such as Gazelles with Truffles, Terfez Tajine in Red Sauce, and Truffles with Meatballs. *Terfez* can be bought in food stores in Morocco in cans, though they are not particularly cheap.

Tricastin

Tricastin is the main truffle-growing region of France and it is also the country's main producer of fragrant herbs—lavender, thyme, sage, and rosemary. It is a triangular region in Provence stretching between the towns of Montélimar (famous

Above: Terfez.
Right: Tricastin at the foot of Mont Ventoux, seen from the Château of Suze-la-Rousse.

for its nougat), Orange, and Nyons. This small area, a former papal enclave, covers fifteen communes in the département of Vaucluse and sixty-eight in that of Drôme. Truffles from Tricastin have been entitled to the appellation "Tricastin black truffle" since 1978. By contrast, the "Périgord black truffle" no more has to come from Périgord* than the Brussels sprout does from Belgium, and until the 1978 ruling, all black truffles* (*Tuber melanosporum*) in France were given this name. The French truffle-growers' union is attempting to obtain an AOC (*Appellation d'Origine Contrôlée*) for the truffle.

Tricastin is a land of stony soil and bright sunshine, in the heart of southern France, where the truffle is one of the main industries. Its capital is the town of Saint-Paul-Trois-Châteaux, where there is a handsome Romanesque cathedral in pure Provençal style and, close by, a museum devoted to the truffle. A permanent exhibition covers the nine well-known European species but pays particular attention to the black truffle. There are videos featuring the truffle's life cycle*, its special properties, truffle-hunting, and the marketing* process. Also on offer at the museum are wines from the slopes of the Tricastin hills—wines with a lively and elegant nose. A big truffle fair is held in the town on the second Sunday in February, and there is a weekly market on Tuesday morning, starting at 10:00 a.m. from November through March. The signature dishes of the region all incorporate the fragrance of the Tricastin truffle and the fruity olive oil of Nyons, and are best accompanied by wines from the region.

■ Truffle-fly

Truffle-hunting* by observing the movements of the truffle-fly is practiced mainly by those hunters who have neither dog nor pig to assist them. This method is becoming rarer, but there are still a few people who retain the skill. Eight species of fly lay their eggs in truffles. All are small and reddish and can only fly short distances. They have an acute sense of smell and always land on a spot beneath which is buried a truffle. The flies lay their eggs in the truffle so that the larvae have a ready source of food when they hatch. Spotting a truffle by watching for the fly requires not only an experienced eye but also exemplary patience. The weather needs to be just right—cloudy, even slightly misty—and the soil temperature needs to be higher than 42°F (5°C). When the flies can be seen on the truffle-ground*, truffle-hunting can begin. The best time of day is between 11:00 a.m. and 4:00 p.m. Hunters carefully scrutinize the ground, with their back to the sun, so that they can spot the flies that hover or remain stationary at the foot of the truffle-bearing trees. They must then move forward in complete silence, sweeping the ground a few inches in front of their feet using a long hazelnut switch, so as to be able to locate the exact spot from which truffle-flies will rise when disturbed. They then stick a small wooden marker into the soil at that point. If they cannot determine the precise location, they must wait patiently for the fly to return and reposition itself over the truffle. When several truffles have been located in this manner, it is essential to sniff the earth to check for the presence

The truffle-fly.

of a truffle before digging it up. Since this method of hunting truffles is so time-consuming, it is more of a curiosity nowadays than a genuine harvesting technique.

Truffle-ground

The truffle-ground or trufflebed is the place where truffles are harvested, but it is also an ecological entity that embodies various factors essential for its growth. A productive truffleground requires a perfect balance between the fungus and the various factors that make up its environment, such as the soil*, climate (seasons*), host, and fauna and flora. The balance must be maintained, or the plantation will stop producing truffles. The truffle is a demanding fungus: it not only requires a specific environment in which to flourish, but also needs special nurturing. The ideal truffleground is situated on a gentle slope, protected from the prevailing winds, where the ground benefits from a favorable microclimate with plenty of sunshine. There are two types of truffleground, natural and artificial.

Planting truffle-bearing saplings.

The former is the product of the evolution of the ecosystem and is found in woods or beside footpaths and always develops at the cost of the surrounding vegetation. Production in these patches soon diminishes due to a lack of maintenance. The second type is the result of human intervention, by planting acorns or young trees. Other crops can be grown alongside truffles, notably grape vines and lavender. In both cases, the aim is to bridge the period of several years between the planting and the development of the truffle-ground, to provide a source of

income for the farmer in the interval. Planting is always done in winter. Not until ten or more years later will the first burnt patches* begin to appear, provided that the young trees are allowed to develop properly and the area is kept well-tended. Two or three years after the appeareance of the patches, truffles can be harvested. At the time of writing, about eighty per-cent of French production came from artificial truffle-grounds, although the secretive nature of the truffle harvest makes statis-tics in this area somewhat unre-liable.

A cultivated truffle-ground in the Lalbenque region.

Selling white truffles.

White Truffles

Truffles are generally classified as white or black. The term "white truffle" takes on a different meaning, depending on whether one is in Italy* or France*. In Italy, there is no other expression but *tartufo bianco* to indicate the white *Tuber magnatum Pico*. This truffle, also known as the Piedmont or Alba truffle, also grows in parts of Slovenia and Croatia. Because it is very specific to damp but well-aerated soils, it does not grow in France, where the soil is heavier. The main regions in which it grows are Piedmont, Tuscany, the Marches, I Molise (which alone accounts for forty percent of national production), and Umbria. The *ascocarp* (fruiting-body) can grow quite large, from one to six inches. The truffle bears a superficial resemblance to a potato. The peridium is dirty yellow or stone colored, smooth and devoid of warts or excrescences. The gleba is yellowish and shot through with small white veins that turn red when exposed to the air. It has a powerful fragrance (though nothing like that of the Périgord truffle), which is a mixture of garlic, shallot, parmesan, and gas, which the French gastronome Brillat-Savarin described as "a slight taste of garlic which does nothing to harm its perfection because it does not produce any disagreeable aftertaste."

The white truffle ripens in the fall. It currently grows only in the wild, although Italy has invested a great deal of money in planting truffle-bearing trees. The best trees for the purpose are lime, hazel, sessile oak, and poplar. Each type of tree produces a slightly different coloration in the flesh, varying from pale chestnut to hazelnut, but the difference is subtle. The white truffle is ruined by cooking, which destroys its fragrance, so it is always eaten raw. Its powerful flavor is enhanced by hot food, however, such as pasta and risotto, but it does not do well in strongly-flavored sauces and cooked dishes. In restaurants, diners are presented with the truffle and a grater so that they can grate truffle shavings over the food. The white truffle is exported to Japan, France, and the United States, where there is a substantial Italian community.

The only similar truffle is *Tuber borchii*, about which there is little information as to production. *T. borchii* is known in France as the white spring truffle or the common white truffle, and there are Italians who call it *bianchetto* ("little white") or *marzuolo* (March truffle). There is another white-fleshed truffle that grows in different European countries: the summer truffle* (*Tuber aestivum*) or St John's truffle, which the Italians call "summer white truffle" or "sun truffle." However, this truffle has a black skin and is a subject of trickery, because its flesh can be artificially darkened, enabling it to be passed it off as the black truffle*. Italy is the only country that produces the white truffle, with the exception of a few acres in Slovenia and Croatia (once part of Italy, and whose truffles are exported to Italy). The truffle is produced throughout the northern half of the peninsula, in Piedmont and Liguria, Tuscany, the Marches, Lombardy, and elsewhere. *T. magnatum* fruits easily in a variety of soils and in various locations, yet all attempts to transplant it elsewhere have failed, since it likes only light, aerated soils and dislikes the damp. Since the 1930s, the city of Alba* in Piedmont has fêted the white truffle with a big annual festival. Italians are utterly devoted to their white truffle—after all, they say, in music one white note is worth at least two black ones!

Tuber magnatum Pico.

▮ Winter Truffles

There are three species of winter truffle: the black truffle*, the musky truffle*, and the Chinese truffle*.

Tuber melanosporum—the black Périgord, Tricastin, or Norcia truffle (the latter name is given to it in Umbria, Italy), is the most famous of the truffles, known for its intense and very special fragrance and its delicious flavor. The peridium consists of pyramid-shaped scales,

Tuber brumale is known as the black winter truffle or musky truffle. The peridium is blackish and detaches easily from the gray-black flesh, which is shot through with white veins. Unlike the black truffle, these veins never change color but remain white. The aroma and flavor are rather unpleasant. The related species *Tuber moschatum* smells of grass. These truffles are also harvested from November through March

which are reddish at first then black at maturity, and the gleba is blackish-violet, shot through with fine white veins that eventually turn red. It is harvested during the traiditonal truffle season from November through March, and has a powerful aroma, reminiscent of mushrooms and hazelnuts. It grows wild in southeastern and southwestern France*, and in Spain* and Italy*. France has the largest production, amounting to around forty metric tons a year.

The musky truffle.

in the same places as the black truffle, but cost half the price of *T. melanosporum*. They can be used cooked.

Tuber indicum, known as the Chinese truffle, looks very similar to *T. melanosporum* but lacks its powerful fragrance. The peridium is black and warty and the gleba is shot through with many veins. *T. indicum* has little odor and flavor at the best of times, but since it is usually transported in unsuitable conditions and gathered while still immature, it reaches the consumer virtually flavorless.

The fungus is found in China in the provinces of Yunnan and Sechuan and it is harvested from December through March. The price ranges between US$25 and US$35 per pound.

whether grown in the southwest or the southeast, but the climate, soil, fauna and flora will alter the fragrance. There are wines whose bouquet is similar to that of the truffle, a feature that can be discerned in certain vintages of Châteauneuf-du-Pape.

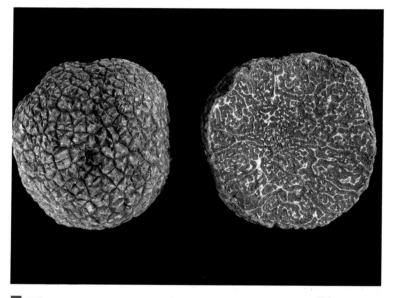

■ Wines

There is no intention here of trying to compete with the recommendations of wine experts, but merely of discussing the best wines to drink with truffles, a particularly delicate matter. Dishes accompanied by truffles need not be elaborate or prestigious, but can be simple, such as a bowl of good pasta, and the truffle is best served raw or merely warmed through. The wine should not be allowed to mask the aroma but should be complementary to it. The best wine to choose is probably one produced in truffle-growing country, where the soil is stony, sandy or clay, and where there is plenty of undergrowth. The black truffle* is the same species,

The same aroma is present in Vieux Cahors, the great Médocs or the best Saint-Émilion vintages, as well as in Pomerol wines. The spiciness of a Côte-rôtie, or an Hermitage Blanc, with its hazelnut fragrance, will also harmonize well with the truffle. Nor should the Côteaux du Tricastin wines be forgotten, in which the Syrah grape variety predominates and which, if served at room temperature, are the natural allies of the truffle. If raw truffle peelings are served as part of the appetizer, an excellent champagne will add a festive note to the aperitif and turn every celebration into a great occasion.

In Piedmont and Alba*, in the Italian fall, the truffle fragrance

Tuber melanosporum.

Wine, truffles, and foie gras.

mingles in the air with bunches of Dolcetto and Nebbiolo grapes, and the dry wines they produce combine well with the white truffle. The hills of the Langhe are planted alternately with Barolo and Barbaresco grapevines. The delicate body of the Barbaresco and heartiness of the Barolo go well with black truffles. The combination of truffles and wine with typical local farmhouse cheeses, such as Murazzano and Toma d'Alba of the Upper Langhe, is a happy one.

■ Work

Many people earn their living from the truffle, most of them working in agriculture. In the case of cultivated truffles, there is a lot to do. Someone must plant the seedlings or saplings and someone must see to the weeding, trimming, and watering. There is the truffle-hound* to train, and then there are the human truffle-hunters* and the people who take the truffles to the market to be sold, though this work is seasonal. Finally, there is the whole preserving* operation, which involves cooking and canning or bottling.

The truffle-grower, whether in France*, Italy*, or the United States, requires patience, perseverance, and tenacity, because it takes from ten to fifteen years before a tree yields its first harvest. Dedication is therefore required. Production depends very much on the experimentation* centres engaged in trying to unravel the mystery of the truffle fruiting process.

The broker* is the key figure in truffle-buying, acting as the intermediary between the grower and the dealer or canner, or being employed exclusively by a canner.

Truffle preserving is usually a traditional family business. Like the broker, truffle preservers need to know a great deal about truffles and the workings of the trade. They must acquire the skill to recognize the various species by their smell and to tell which region they came from. They have to be able to grade truffles, fresh or sterilized, and import or export the fresh or canned species that are permitted to be traded commercially, according to the rules laid down in the relevant legislation.

Finally, there are the master chefs, those magicians who have progressively developed the beliefs around this mysterious mushroom.

Whatever role they play, all these people are truffle enthusiasts, who love to feel the rough skin of the fungus as they rub it between their fingers: the magic, secret, sacred truffle that is the supreme reward for their labors.

Teaching truffle-hunting.

"The most learned men have been questioned as to the nature of this tuber, and after two thousand years of argument and discussion their answer is the same as it was on the first day: we do not know. The truffles themselves have been interrogated, and have answered simply: eat us and praise the Lord."

Alexandre Dumas, *Grand Dictionnaire de cuisine*

BLACK TRUFFLE OPEN-FACED SANDWICH
1 fresh black truffle, ½ cup olive oil, ½ teaspoon sea salt, 4 slices whole-grain bread

Clean the truffle and slice it thinly. Marinate the slices in the olive oil, and sprinkle with salt. Lightly toast the slices of bread, cover them with the slices of truffle, and eat as soon as possible, with the wine of your choice.

SERVES 2

SLIVERS OF FRESH TRUFFLE WITH SALT
1 fresh truffle, salt, olive oil

Cut slivers of truffle with a truffle grater or a very sharp knife, and place them in a dish lined with a clean cloth. Sprinkle with salt (*fleur de sel* is best, if you can get it) and taste. Add a drizzle of olive oil if desired.

SERVES 4

TRUFFLE OIL
1 oz. black truffles, 1-quart bottle olive oil

Requires advance preparation.

Brush and wipe the truffles carefully with a damp cloth. Dry well. Peel them, and then finely chop the peel. Warm the olive oil, add the truffle peel shavings and one whole truffle. Keep the other truffles in a hermetically sealed container in the refrigerator. Leave the oil to infuse in the refrigerator for at least twenty-four hours before use. This oil is delicious with broiled or grilled fish or meats or with potatoes.

MAKES ONE QUART TRUFFLE OIL

WHITE ASPARAGUS WITH TRUFFLE OIL
1 bunch white as-paragus (about 10 oz.), 1 truffle weigh-ing about 1½ oz., walnut oil, olive oil, balsamic vinegar, 1 shallot, fleur de sel, freshly ground pep-per, chervil

Make the sauce a day in advance. Blend two-thirds of the walnut oil with one-third olive oil, add the finely chopped shallot, salt and pepper to taste, a teaspoon of balsamic vinegar, and the grated truffle. Leave to marinate overnight. Cook the asparagus in boiling, salted water. When tender, remove from the water, drain well, and serve with the sauce drizzled over the spears. Sprinkle with chervil just before serving.

SERVES 4

POTATO AND TRUFFLE SALAD

2 truffles, the same volume of shallots, 2 potatoes (waxy varieties are best), truffle oil (prepared at least a day ahead of time), salt, freshly ground black pepper

Remove the oil from the refrigerator and let it to come to room temperature. Boil or steam the potatoes in their skins. Slice the truffles thinly and mince or grate them so that they constitute a purée. Once the potatoes are tender, peel them while still hot, cut them into thick rounds, and arrange them on the plates. Pour a thin stream of truffle oil over them, and sprinkle with truffle slices and the shallot purée. Season to taste with salt and pepper.

SERVES 4–6

TRUFFLE SALAD WITH PUMPKIN

1 truffle (approx. 1 oz.), 1 cup fresh pumpkin cubes, 2 cups washed, drained Bibb lettuce or mâche, 4 tablespoons olive oil, 1 teaspoon hazelnut oil, 1 teaspoon lemon juice, a few drops of balsamic vinegar, 1 pinch ground cinnamon, salt, pepper

Sauté the pumpkin for five minutes in one tablespoon of the olive oil. Season with salt, pepper, and a pinch of cinnamon. Remove from the heat and sprinkle with the hazelnut oil. Leave to cool. Slice the truffle and mix with lemon juice, two tablespoons of the oil, a pinch of salt, and a turn of the pepper mill. Mix one tablespoon of the olive oil with the lemon juice. Arrange the lettuce on two serving plates and dress with the lemon-oil mixture. Place the pumpkin cubes in the center of each dish and cover with truffle slices. Add a dash of oil and a few drops of balsamic vinegar. Serve with slices of toast and a bottle of olive oil on the side.

SERVES 4

CRISPY GARLIC CHOY SUM WITH BLACK TRUFFLES

1 large head choy sum cabbage, washed and cut into 2-inch pieces, 2 tbsp oil, 16 garlic cloves, sliced thinly, 1 cup chicken broth, 1 large black truffle, sliced (shiitake and truffle oil can be substituted), salt, black pepper

Heat the oil in a wok. Brown the sliced garlic. Add the choy sum and season with salt and pepper. Add chicken broth and stir-fry for only 3 minutes. Serve

immediately and cover with truffle slices. The steam from the dish will heat the truffle, enabling it to release its oil and flavor. If using shiitake, add them after the garlic, before adding the choy sum. Sprinkle with truffle oil before serving.
SERVES 4

CHESTNUTS AND FIGS WITH VINAIGRETTE AND TRUFFLE

1 pound whole chestnuts, 6 black mission figs, 8 oz. chestnut honey, 6 oz. truffle, 8 oz. Bibb lettuce or mâche, 4 bamboo skewers (pre-soaked in water)

VINAIGRETTE
1 shallot, 2 teaspoons fresh thyme, ½ cup white wine vinegar, ½ cup extra virgin olive oil, 1 teaspoon Dijon mustard, salt and pepper to taste

Rinse the chestnuts under water. Take a sharp knife and score the flat side of the chestnut with a cross. Toss chestnuts in a little oil and sprinkle with salt. Lay the oiled nuts out on a baking sheet and roast in a pre-heated 275-degree oven for about 20 minutes or until fully roasted; the shell will open. Let the chestnuts cool, then peel and chop half of the chestnuts finely and the other half coarsely.

Slice the figs in half and place on skewers with three halves per skewer. Place the skewers on a baking sheet and drizzle with honey. Sprinkle the finely chopped chestnuts over the figs and broil them under a hot broiler until browned. To make the dressing, combine the shallots, mustard, vinegar, and thyme and whisk together. Slowly whisk in the oil, finishing with the truffle oil, and season with salt and pepper. To serve, dress the lettuce with the vinaigrette, sprinkle with finely chopped chestnuts and place in the center of the plate. Place a warm fig skewer diagonally on top of each salad serving. Decorate each plate with coarsely chopped chestnuts. Finely slice the truffle and lay on top of the fig salad. Drizzle truffle vinaigrette around the plate.

SERVES 6–8

BLACK TRUFFLE PASTA

1 pound capellini, 1¾ cups frozen peas, ¼ stick unsalted butter, ½ oz. chopped black truffle, 1½ oz. black truffle oil, 1 teaspoon champagne vinegar, 1 small minced shallot, 1 bunch chives, finely minced

Cook pasta in a large pot of salted boiling water until *al dente* (6 to 7 minutes). Add peas and continue cooking about 1 minute. Drain well and toss in butter, truffle vinaigrette (made by combining ½ oz. chopped black truffle, 1½ oz. black truffle oil, 1 teaspoon champagne vinegar, and 1 small minced shallot), and chives. Season and serve.

SERVES 4

RISOTTO WITH BLACK OR WHITE TRUFFLES

1 fresh truffle, 1 large onion, minced, 4 cups risotto rice, 1 tbsp butter, 2 tbsp olive oil, 2 tbsp vegetable oil, 3¾ cups meat broth, ¾ cup grated parmesan, salt and pepper

Sauté the onion in a blend of the two oils. Add the rice and stir until the grains are translucent. Add all but half a cup of the broth and stir. When the liquid has been absorbed (about 20 minutes), add the rest of the broth and season to taste. Just before serving, add the butter and parmesan, mix well, and scatter with slivers of truffle.

SERVES 6

PURÉE OF CELERY ROOT AND RICE WITH TRUFFLES

1 truffle, 2 tablespoons truffle oil, two-thirds celery root, rice, 1 quart milk, light cream, sea salt and pepper

Peel and dice the celery root. Cook for twenty minutes in salted water. Meanwhile, cook the rice, which should be equal in volume to half of the celery root, in boiling, salted water for 10 minutes: it should be barely tender.

Drain the rice and return it to the pan. Finish cooking the rice in the milk. When the rice and celery root are cooked, drain and blend them in a mixer. Season to taste, and add the cream in a thin stream, stirring until the desired consistency is obtained. Just before serving, sprinkle with truffle oil and beat again. Peel the truffle and sprinkle shavings over the purée. Serve with poultry or game.

SERVES 4

WHITE TRUFFLE POLENTA

1 cup partially precooked polenta, ⅔ cup grated parmesan, ¼ cup butter, 2 tablespoons olive oil, 1 raw white truffle, 2 tsp table salt, freshly ground black pepper

Bring four cups of salted water to the boil. Pour the polenta in gradually, continuously stirring, then beat well for about five minutes. The polenta is cooked when it detaches itself from the sides of the pot. Turn off the heat and season with salt and pepper. Mix well and pour into a bowl. Cover with truffle shavings and sprinkle with a little olive oil. Polenta should be made at the last moment and eaten warm.

SERVES 4

TRUFFLED CHICKEN
(POULARDE DEMI-DEUIL)

1 large roasting chicken, 1 fresh truffle (about ¾ oz.), truffle juice, 4 carrots, 2 turnips, 2 leeks, salt, 1 piece of cheesecloth

Dress the chicken several hours in advance. To do this, slice the truffle thinly and slip the slices under the chicken skin of the breast and thighs. Wrap the bird tightly in cheesecloth and tie the wings and thighs with string. Peel the vegetables and place them in a deep pot or casserole. Cover with water and add salt. Bring the liquid to the boil and add the chicken. It should be barely covered with water. Cover the pot and cook for 1 hour on low heat. Leave the chicken to cool in the broth, then drain and degrease the broth. Serve the chicken with a risotto made from the broth and flavored with the truffle juice.

SERVES 6

SCALLOP CARPACCIO

2 oz. black Périgord truffles, 12 raw scallops, olive oil, 1 shallot, sea salt, freshly ground black pepper

Place individual dishes in the refrigerator to chill for a few minutes. Cut the white parts of the scallops away from the shell, using a pointed knife. Chop the shallot. Slice the truffles thinly. Remove the dishes from the refrigerator. Arrange the scallops on them, sprinkle them with the chopped shallot, and arrange the slices of truffle over them. Salt and pepper and sprinkle with olive oil.

SERVES 4

CODDLED EGGS WITH WHITE TRUFFLES

Use one egg per person. Break an egg into each ramekin. Sprinkle with salt and pepper and add slivers of truffle. Cover with a saucer or a cloth and leave for 10 minutes at room temperature. Place the ramekins in a steamer and steam for 3 minutes.

SCRAMBLED EGGS WITH BLACK TRUFFLES

1 oz. black truffles, slivered, 6 eggs, olive oil, sea salt, freshly ground black pepper

Beat the eggs in a bowl with 1 tablespoon water. Heat the oil in a saucepan and add the eggs, stirring until set. Sprinkle with salt and pepper and add slivers of truffle. Serve with crusty French loaf and farmhouse butter.

SERVES 3

SELECTED BIBLIOGRAPHY

Alford, Katherine. *Caviar, Truffles and Foie Gras: Recipes of Divine Indulgence.* San Francisco: Chronicle Books, 2001.

Barnhart, Harley E. "Truffling Along." In *Mushroom, the Journal of Wild Mushrooming,* Vol. 8, No. 3; Summer, 1985. Issue 8: 8–13.

Barnhart, Harley E. "You can read about black truffles in English." In *Mushroom, The Journal of Wild Mushrooming,* Vol. 13, No. 3; Summer, 1995. Issue 48: 24–26.

Boyd, Jim "Truffles Come from Different Continents." In *Mushroom, the Journal of Wild Mushrooming,* Vol. 13, No. 3; Summer, 1995. Issue 48: 19–21

Dorn, Larry. "Raising American Truffles." In *Organic Gardening,* Oct. 1987, pp. 24–27.

Hall, Ian; Brown, Gordon & Byars, James. *The Black Truffle: Its History, Uses, and Cultivation,* Crop & Food Research, Christchurch, New Zealand, 1994.

Jaros, Patrick. *The Joy of Truffles Cookbook.* New York: Taschen, 1999.

Osler, Mirabel. *The Elusive Truffle.* London: Black Swan, 2000.

Peer, Elizabeth. "On the Trail of the Truffle." *Geo,* Vol. 2, Nov. 1980, pp. 112–130.

Rocchia, Michel. *Truffles: The Black Diamond and Other Kinds,* Avignon: Barthelemy, 1992.

Useful addresses

North American Truffling Society
P.O. Box 269
Corvallis, OR 97339, USA
Tel.: (503) 752-2243

North American Mycological Society
10 Lynn Brooke Place
Charleston, WV 25312-9521, USA
Tel.: (304) 744-1654
www.namyco.org

British Mycological Society
Joseph Banks Building
Royal Botanic Gardens
Kew, Surrey TW9 3AB, UK
Tel.: 020 8332 5720
www.bms.ac.uk

**The Confrérie de la Truffe de
Bourgogne**, France
Organizes truffle-dog trials annually.
Tel.: 03 80 61 05 31

Truffle markets
and festivals

UNITED STATES
White Truffle Festival
Annual truffle event, held in various
cities across the United States.
Tel.: (888) 662-6442
www.italmangia.com

ITALY
Alba
Truffle festival held in November
every year.
Tourist Office:
Tel.: 0173 35833

FRANCE
Aups
Truffle Day
Last Sunday in January.
Market from late November
through late February on Thursday
mornings from 10:00 a.m. in the
Place Frédéric Mistral.
Tel.: 04 94 70 0080

Carpentras
Truffle market
From November through March
on Friday mornings
from 8:00 a.m. through 10:00 a.m.
Tourist office:
Tel.: 04 90 63 00 78

Drôme
Truffle markets throughout the week
December through March
Monday at Chamaret (10:00 a.m.)
Tuesday at Grigan and Saint-Paul-
Trois-Chateaux (10:00 a.m.)
Wednesday at Valéras (10:00 a.m.)
Thursday at Nyons and Montségur-
Sur-Lauzon (10:00 a.m.)
Friday at Suze-la Rousse (11:00 a.m.)
Saturday at Richerenches (10:00 a.m.)
Sunday at Taulignan (11:00 a.m.)

Lalbenque
Truffle market on Tuesday
afternoons, from 2:00 p.m.
through 3:00 p.m.
November through March
Competition for the best basket of
truffles, late January
Tel.: 05 65 31 50 08

Limogne-en-Quercy
Friday mornings from November
through March.
Tel.: 05 65 31 50 01

Paris
National Truffle Day
Held annually in early February
Tel: 01 42 36 03 29

Richerenches
Saturday market
November through March
Truffle Mass celebrated in honor
of Saint Anthony with a parade of
the Confrérie du Diamant Noir in
ceremonial dress on the third
Sunday in January
Tel.: 04 90 28 02 00

The town of Carpentras.

BUYER'S GUIDE

Where to buy truffles

Earthy Delights
1161 E. Clark Road, Suite 260
DeWitt, MI 48820
USA
Tel.: (800) 367-4709

Fresh Truffles
258 Belsize Road
London NW6 4BT
England
sales@freshtruffles.com

Garland Gourmet Truffles
3020 Ode Turner Road
Hillsborough, NC 27278
USA
Tel.: (919) 732-3041
www.garlandtruffles.com

Pippin's Maison des Truffes
331 Aaron Circle
Durham, NC 27713
USA
Tel.: (919) 361-9622

Plantin America Truffles
518 Gregory Avenue
Suite B208
Weehawken, NJ 07087
USA
Tel.: (201) 867-4590

The Truffle Market
P.O. Box 4234
Gettysburg, PA 17325
USA
Tel.: (800) 822-4003
www.trufflemarket.com

Fortnum and Mason
181 Piccadilly
London W1A 1ER
England
Tel.: 0207 734 8040
www.fortnumandmason.com

Restaurants with truffle menus
As truffle menus are often proposed only in season, you are advised to ring ahead and check the menu is available.

UNITED STATES
Arcodoro
5000 Westheimer Road
Houston, TX 77056
Tel.: (713) 621-6888

La Toque
1140 Rutherford Cross Road
Rutherford, CA 94573
Tel.: (707) 963-9770
www.latoque.com

Water's Edge Restaurant
44th Drive
Long Island City, NY 11101
Tel.: (718) 482-0033

UNITED KINGDOM
Aubergine
11 Park Walk
London SW10 0AJ
Tel.: 020 7352 3449

Brown's Hotel
Albemarle Street
London W1
Tel.: 020 7493 6020

The Ritz Hotel
150 Picadilly
London W1V 9DG
Tel.: 0207 300 2308

FRANCE
Château de Rochegude
26790 Rochegude
Tel.: 04 75 97 21 10

L'Oustalet
Place de la Mairie
84190 Gigondas
Tel.: 04 90 65 85 30

I N D E X

The authors wish to express their warmest thanks to the
Henras and Pierre Sourzat companies.

Photographic credits: AKG, PARIS: 6, 12–13, 20; Franck Bel: 4–5, 8–9, 10, 11, 14–15, 16,
19, 22–23, 28–29, 31, 45, 49, 50, 54, 64, 72, 74, 93, 114; Pierre Sourzat: 17, 24, 25, 27,
30, 32, 33, 34–35, 36, 37, 38, 39, 40–41, 42, 43, 44, 47, 50, 52, 53, 56–57, 58, 59, 62, 63,
65, 66, 67, 68, 70-71, 75, 83, 84–85, 86–87, 88, 92, 93, 94, 95, 97, 98–99, 100, 101, 102,
103, 104, 105, 106–107, 115; Béatriz Garrigo: 26; Giraudon: 78–79; Pierre Ferbos/Société
Mycologique de France: 91; Édition Édisud: 76–77; collection Simone Mathieu: 82;
Collection Henras: 64–65; Reseachers/John Foster 61; Terre du Sud/Philippe Giraud: 36.

Quotations: pages 50, 105: translated from Alexandre Dumas, *Grand Dictionnaire de cuisine*
(Paris: Phébus, 2000); page 64: translated from Edmond Rostand, *Cyrano de Bergerac* (Paris:
Gallimard, 1983); page 75: translated from Sidonie-Gabrielle Colette, *Prisons et paradis*
(Paris: Fayard, 1986).

Recipes: page 109 - Slivers of fresh truffle with salt / White asparagus with truffle oil, page 110 -
Risotto with black or white truffles: translated from Françoise Dubarry, *Les Marchés du Sud*
(Paris: Editions de l'Épure, 2001); page 109 - Truffle oil / page 110 - Potato and truffle salad
/ page 112 - Purée of celery root and rice with truffles: translated from Jean-Louis Ménage
and Philippe Bucquet, *La Truffe, 10 façons de la préparer* (Paris: Editions de l'Épure, 1996);
page 110 Crispy garlic choy sum with black truffles: Recipe Courtesy of Ming Tsai; page 110 -
Chestnut roasted figs with truffle vinaigrette: Recipe Courtesy of Don Pintabona, Executive Chef,
Tribeca Grill; page 112 - Black truffle pasta: Recipe Courtesy of Kerry Hefferman.

Translated and adapted from the French by Josephine Bacon
Copy-editing: Corinne Orde
Typesetting: Julie Houis, À Propos
Color separation: Pollina S.A., France

Originally published as *L'ABCdaire des truffes* © 2001 Flammarion
English-language edition © 2001 Flammarion

ISBN: 2-08010-627-9
N° d'édition: FA0627-01-VII
Dépôt légal: 10/2001
Printed and bound by Pollina S.A., France n° L84571